THE
PROVIDENCE
OF
GOD

PAUL HELM

CONTOURS *of*

CHRISTIAN

THEOLOGY

GERALD BRAY
Series Editor

INTERVARSITY PRESS
DOWNERS GROVE, ILLINOIS 60515

© 1993 by Paul Helm

Published in the United States of America by InterVarsity Press, Downers Grove, Illinois, with permission from Universities and Colleges Christian Fellowship, Leicester, England.

All rights reserved. No part of this book may be reproduced in any form without written permission from InterVarsity Press, P.O. Box 1400, Downers Grove, Illinois 60515.

InterVarsity Press® is the book-publishing division of InterVarsity Christian Fellowship®, a student movement active on campus at hundreds of universities, colleges and schools of nursing in the United States of America, and a member movement of the International Fellowship of Evangelical Students. For information about local and regional activities, write Public Relations Dept., InterVarsity Christian Fellowship, 6400 Schroeder Rd., P.O. Box 7895, Madison, WI 53707-7895.

Unless otherwise stated, quotations from the Bible are taken from the British edition of the HOLY BIBLE: NEW INTERNATIONAL VERSION®, NIV®. Copyright ©1973, 1978 and 1984 by the International Bible Society. Used by permission of Zondervan Publishing House. All rights reserved.

ISBN 0-8308-1533-3

Printed in the United States of America ∞

Library of Congress Cataloging-in-Publication Data

Helm, Paul.
    The providence of God/Paul Helm.
      p.   cm.—(Contours of Christian theology)
    Includes bibliographical references.
    ISBN 0-8308-1533-3 (alk. paper)
    1. Providence and government of God.   I. Title. II. Series.
  BT135.H35 1994
  231'.5—dc20   93-40938
                                             CIP

----

17   16   15   14   13   12   11   10
08

For Robert

Sov'reign Ruler of the skies,
Ever gracious, ever wise;
All my times are in thy hand,
All events at thy command.

His decree who form'd the earth
Fix'd my first and second birth;
Parents, native place, and time,
All appointed were by him.

He that form'd me in the womb,
He shall guide me to the tomb;
All my times shall ever be
Order'd by his wise decree.

Times of sickness; times of health;
Times of penury and wealth;
Times of trial and of grief;
Times of triumph and relief;

Times the tempter's power to prove;
Times to taste the Saviour's love
All must come, and last, and end,
As shall please my heavenly Friend.

Plagues and deaths around me fly;
Till he bids, I cannot die;
Not a single shaft can hit,
Till the God of love sees fit.

John Ryland (1753–1825)

Contents

Series Preface

Contours of Christian Theology covers the main themes of Christian doctrine. The series offers a systematic presentation of most of the major doctrines in a way which complements the traditional textbooks but does not copy them. Top priority has been given to contemporary issues, some of which may not be dealt with elsewhere from an evangelical point of view. The series aims, however, not merely to answer current objections to evangelical Christianity, but also to rework the orthodox evangelical position in a fresh and compelling way. The overall thrust is therefore positive and evangelistic in the best sense.

The series is intended to be of value to theological students at all levels, whether at a Bible college, a seminary or a secular university. It should also appeal to ministers and to educated lay-people. As far as possible, efforts have been made to make technical vocabulary accessible to the non-specialist reader, and the presentation has avoided the extremes of academic style. Occasionally this has meant that particular issues have been presented without a thorough argument, taking into account different positions, but when this has happened, authors have been encouraged to refer the reader to other works which take the discussion further. For this purpose adequate but not exhaustive notes have been provided.

The doctrines covered in the series are not exhaustive, but have been chosen in response to contemporary concerns. The title and general presentation of each volume are at the discretion of the author, but final editorial decisions have been taken by the Series Editor in consultation with IVP.

In offering this series to the public, the authors and the publishers hope that it will meet the needs of theological students in this generation, and bring honour and glory to God the Father, and to his Son, Jesus Christ, in whose service the work has been undertaken from the beginning.

Gerald Bray
Series Editor

Preface

Parts of this book were written during my tenure of a Summer Fellowship at the H. H. Meeter Center for Calvin Studies, Calvin College and Seminary, Grand Rapids, Michigan, during 1991. I am grateful for the opportunity for scholarly work that this Fellowship provided.

A small section of chapter 2 first saw the light of day as part of 'The Impossibility of Divine Passibility' in *The Power and Weakness of God*, ed. Nigel M. de S. Cameron (Edinburgh: Rutherford House, 1990). Parts of chapter 6 are taken from 'Asking God' (*Themelios*, September 1986) and 'Prayer and Providence' in *Christian Faith and Philosophical Theology*, ed. Gijsbert van den Brink, Luco J. van den Brom and Marcel Sarot (Kampen: Pharos, 1992). Thanks are due to the respective editors and publishers of this material for permission to recycle it here.

I am particularly grateful to the editor of this series, Gerald Bray, for his support and advice, and to the publishers for various kinds of help. Together they have added considerably to the pleasure that writing the book has brought.

Paul Helm

Introduction

Anyone who attempts to limn the contours of a Christian doctrine has a choice. Either he can set differing versions of the doctrine side by side with Olympian detachment, or he can offer a view of his own.

In this book I offer a view of my own, though not one that is peculiar to me. The chief reason for this approach is to try to avoid the blandness and obliqueness that often come from setting one view beside another in a 'neutral' way. For an author to offer a view of his own carries with it the hope of putting readers on their mettle by inviting them to take sides and to think out their own views in dialogue with the one that is proffered on the pages before them.

In what follows, I put forward the 'no-risk' view of divine providence, a view which I believe corresponds both to Scripture and to the historic teaching of the church. I have supported this view with arguments, and have denied the cogency of other arguments sometimes used in its support. Obviously, this procedure will not commend itself to everyone who agrees with the conclusion, much less to those who take the view that God takes risks. I have, of course, attempted to keep faith with Scripture and with the classical Christian theological tradition that is grounded in it.

The question is whether this view (or its rivals) goes beyond Scripture in saying things that are not warranted by the Bible's teaching. Such a possibility could be minimized, if not avoided altogether, by practising negative theology. Negative theology is a necessary element in Christian theology and undoubtedly has its advantages. To say that God is immortal and invisible, while it tells us what God is not, says nothing about what God *is*. This is both necessary and safe. But a wholly negative theology is ultimately sterile.

Because Scripture is not a library of books in systematic theology, any systematic presentation of a scriptural doctrine invites the charge that it goes beyond the text. In this vein both the orthodox view of the person of Christ, and the doctrine of the Trinity, have at different times been said to add to Scripture. After all, the word 'providence' does not appear in Scripture, not at least in the Authorized Version, any more than does the word 'Trinity'. This book on the providence of God is written in the belief that nothing in it is at odds with Scripture. But since divine providence touches some of the deepest themes – God's sovereignty, human freedom, sin and evil, human tragedy and cosmic disaster – it is likely that any serious treatment will contain controversial elements. Whether this book is controversial in that it goes beyond Scripture in an unacceptable way is for my readers to consider, and I invite them to do so.

1

ORIENTATION

'Divine providence', or even 'the providence of God', appears to be a cold, academic abstraction, a matter of concern only to the systematic theologian or the philosopher rather than to the Christian believer. More than this, the word 'providence' is old-fashioned, and is very rarely used. This may reinforce the view that a discussion of the providence of God such as we are about to begin is a matter of academic or at best of historical interest.

But it would be a mistake to draw this conclusion. For we are embarking on a study of *God's activity now*. Far from studying what is static or abstract, we are to be concerned with God's action in our world, and with how, according to Scripture, that activity is carried out. So we are focusing upon the present, though, as we shall see, God's activity now links with the past (with the plan of God), and with the future (with where the activity of God is leading).

While we are principally dealing with *our* present, the span of time that occupies our lifetimes, it is important not to neglect other 'presents'. For while God's activity is present to us now, that activity was also present to Napoleon in his time, and more importantly to Moses and David and Paul and, of course, to Jesus himself in their times. It would be plausible but nonetheless rash to suppose that the character of God's activity now is the same as it has always been, though this is an assumption made by *deism*. It is one of the important areas of conflict between deism and Christian theism, as we shall see in the next chapter. But it would be unwise to conclude that, because God does not act miraculously now, he can never have done so.

As the word 'providence' indicates, 'the providence of God' is a rather formal way of referring to the fact that God *provides*. And what could be more practical, relevant or down-to-earth than that? In what follows, it may be helpful to keep the idea that God provides continually in mind. For our study will be largely concerned with whom God provides for, what he provides, and how he provides it. In this first chapter we shall begin our treatment by considering the three main contexts in which, according to Scripture, the question of God's providence, his activity now, inevitably arises.

The three contexts

An important part of our faith as Christians is that God cares for us, and that the detail and direction of our lives are under the purposeful control of God. We draw comfort from the fact that nothing is too small to escape the attention of God, nor too minute for him to bother about. We draw inspiration from the fact that God has the power to make difficulties disappear. But we are also aware that often when we pray God does not appear to answer, and that personal tragedy, sickness and bereavement can be allowed by God without any alleviation. Much that happens seems pointless or purposeless. The Lord can take away as well as give, and Christians can receive evil things at his hands as well as good things. In this medley of good and evil, Christians may also be convinced that particular events have occurred as a result of God's direct concern, and so we may come to regard some events in our lives as being particularly 'providential'. In fact, it is highly likely that the average

Christian tends to think that divine providence has to do, not with every detail, but chiefly with special 'providential' occurrences.

Scripture teaches that the love and care of God extend to the details of our lives in a wide variety of ways. For example, in his teaching about care and anxiety, Christ teaches that the hairs of a believer's head are all numbered, and that if every movement of a sparrow is noted by God, believers can be sure that, since they are of more value than many sparrows, their own movements are also directed by God (Mt. 10:29–31). God permitted Paul's thorn in the flesh to remain (2 Cor. 12:7). As characters such as Moses and Joseph looked back on their lives, no doubt they could see how seemingly trivial events – the many-coloured coat, the cry of a baby in the bulrushes, the forgetfulness of a released prisoner – all contributed to the fulfilment of their God-given destiny.

But a moment's thought will show that divine providence surfaces not only in the context of personal issues of this kind. It is not as if the lives of individual Christians are being guided by God and that the rest of the creation is in chaos, each Christian's life being an island of purpose set in a sea of confusion. What is true of the individual is, presumably, true of all other Christians as well – of Christians past, present and future. All these innumerable people are in exactly the same position; God guides them (even when they do not realize it); he cares for them; and, though their lives have a darker side, even pain and loss and heartache are woven by God together with the times of pleasure and blessing to further his purposes for them. When Paul said that 'all things work together for good' (Rom. 8:28, AV), he was referring to the unsurpassable power and wisdom of God that enables him to bring these diverse strands together for the benefit of each Christian and as part of his or her ultimate blessedness.

According to Romans 8, the church was chosen in Christ before the world began, predestined to be conformed to the image of Christ. And as she was predestined for this glorious goal, so her Saviour was predestined by the determinate counsel and foreknowledge of God for the shame and ignominy of the cross, to bear the wrath of God (Acts 2:23). The 'all things' of Romans 8:28 thus refers to all that befalls the Christian church; by some mysterious process God is able to work weakness and persecution and even sin for the good of the church.

So there is more to God's care than the fact that he cares for Christians now. He has cared for them in the past; according to Paul, he cared for him before he was born (Gal. 1:15; cf. Jude 1), and, even more astonishingly, from before the existence of the entire universe. But that care is not only past and present; it extends to the future, to the end of Christians' lives, and to their eternal life beyond the grave, life in the presence of God himself.

God cares for the individual Christian now; but he also cares, has cared, and will care, for all Christians at all times. In some treatments of divine providence, such care for the church is referred to under the heading of 'predestination', the distinction being drawn between the general providence of God over the creation, and the special providence of God as it affects the church. In many respects this is a helpful distinction, because it draws out the fact that the providential purposes have one supreme end, the salvation of the church; it also calls attention to the fact that while God's providence has many different goals, as far as the church of God is concerned there is one goal – conformity to the image of Christ (Rom. 8:29).

Yet there is one important reason for being cautious about emphasizing the contrast between providence and predestination. While the differences mentioned in the previous paragraph are important, the terms we use should not give the impression that God's support and control of his creation as a whole are any less strict and complete than his gracious support and control of his church. Though the one kind of control is often exercised by withholding, and the other by giving, nevertheless God controls all persons and events equally. For this reason no general distinction between predestination and providence will be drawn in what follows. All predestination is providential, and all exercises of providence are predestinarian.

The church of every age, then, has been and is guided by God. But it is possible to go even further. God has created and sustains the whole of the universe. Not only are individual Christians and the Christian church the object of his attention, but so is the whole of nature, together with those forces and people who are indifferent to God and even defiant of him. For God is the creator and the sustainer of all that is. Included in this, according to Scripture, are the hundreds of millions of galaxies, the host of angels and archangels, and Satan himself, as Job learned.

This is, in a way, the most basic relation of all. There can be no doubting God's right, as Creator and Lord of the universe, to govern it in every respect. In many passages of Scripture, God's upholding of the whole of the creation is set forth in detail (*e.g.* Jb. 28 – 40, Pss. 147 – 148). Paul asserted to his Athenian hearers that we 'live and move and have our being' in God (Acts 17:28). All things 'consist' in Christ (Col. 1:17–18, AV). The detail of this superintendence of God over his creation is shown, for example, by the fact that God uses evil people to bring to pass consequences that are unintended by them (Is. 10:7).

God's right to govern what he himself has brought into existence is also emphasized. Like the potter, the Lord has power over the clay; he has the right to do as he pleases with what he has made. It is fundamental to Scripture's vision of God's relation to the universe that 'from him and through him and to him are all things' (Rom. 11:36).

Divine providence is thus bound up with the interests of the individual Christian, with the interests of all Christians – the Christian church – and with the interests of the whole of the creation animate and inanimate. In the remainder of this book we shall refer to these as the *three contexts* of divine providence. No account of divine providence can afford to neglect any one of these contexts, or the relationship between them.

One might go further than this and assert that without a recognition of divine providence it is not possible to understand the biblical view of the Christian life, or of the corporate life of the church, or of the universe as a whole. The three contexts are not insulated from each other, however; they have permeable walls. Since Christians are in the universe that he has created, God could hardly exercise care over them without having control over it.

Can we be more exact about the character of divine providence? In summary, the essential elements of divine providence are these. God *preserves* his creation and all that it contains. This is the most fundamental and basic way in which the care we have referred to is expressed. To preserve is to keep in being or in existence. Having brought the creation into being, God keeps it in being. It does not have an inherent power to sustain itself. But if our idea of divine providence were confined merely to God preserving what he has made, it would be quite inadequate when measured against the biblical data. On this view, God would keep things in existence, but what those things did while existing (what they planned, and how they carried out their plans, for example) would be outside the care of God. He would watch what they did, but nothing more.

God therefore *sustains* his creation. He preserves his creation by sustaining it. While, in any account of providence, justice must be done to divine transcendence, God's separateness from his creation, his sovereignty over it, so divine immanence, his close involvement in creation, must be equally stressed. Not only is every atom and molecule, every thought and desire, kept in being by God, but every twist and turn of each of these is under the direct control of God. He has not, as far as we know, delegated that control to anyone else. The exact nature of this control, insofar as it is possible for us to be exact in such a matter, will occupy us later.

The thought of men and women being directly controlled raises in some minds the spectre of fatalism, of the idea that men and women are blindly destined, perhaps by the stars, for a particular fate irrespective of their own wishes and plans. But such a conception is quite at variance with divine providence. For in providence the controller is not blind, nor is the control exercised apart from what men and women themselves want. The controller is God, who is the supreme purposer of the universe. He exercises his control, as far as men and women are concerned, not apart from what they want to do, or (generally speaking) by compelling them to do what they do not want to do, but through their wills. As Augustine put it:

> Our choices fall within the order of the causes which
> is known for certain to God and is contained in his
> foreknowledge – for, human choices are the causes
> of human acts. It follows that He who foreknew the
> causes of all things could not be unaware that our
> choices were among those causes which were fore-
> known as the causes of our acts.[1]

Divine providence is thus directed, or *purposive*. As we noted
earlier, in bringing to pass the whole matrix of events, and in
sustaining it in all its complexity, God has a certain end or
ends in view. These ends will certainly be accomplished, even
though it is part of the puzzle of divine providence that it is
often extremely difficult to see how what is happening now
contributes to those ends.

The phrase 'end or ends' is used deliberately. From one
point of view God has one end in view, namely the manifest-
ation of his own glory in creation and redemption. This one
end can be further described as, for example, ends regarding
God's justice and goodness. And these ends can be further
refined as they affect particular people in creation, and aspects
of the non-human creation both animate and inanimate.
God's end in providence as far as Mr Smith is concerned may
be quite different from his end for Mrs Robinson or for the
Taj Mahal. But, while these ends differ among themselves,
they all cohere in the one divine purpose, the one end.

What we have seen so far is that there are three contexts in
which questions about divine providence may arise: (1) personal questions of need, of success or failure, or guidance; (2)
the history and destiny of the Christian church, including all
those events which are constitutive of her existence, primarily
the work of Christ and of his Spirit; and (3) the whole of the
animate and inanimate creation in which the life of individuals, and of the church, exists. God's providence is equally
at work in all these areas; there is no sphere in which he is less
in control, or less interested, than in some other sphere, no
'no-go' areas. In each of these contexts God's providence is
exercised in preserving his creatures, in sustaining them
through history, and in directing them to the goals for them
which he has in view.

The following chapters discuss in more detail some of the issues raised by this general picture.

The darker side

The Christian teaching about divine providence asserts that God cares and controls within the three contexts in the ways sketched out above. But there is also a darker side. Christians know that God loves them, and that they may experience God's care. As we have already noted, though, there are also times of personal loss, the experience of forsakenness, of sickness, setbacks, sheer drudgery, and the occurrence of events the purpose of which it seems impossible to fathom. Christians may ask God to guide them and the result may be totally at odds with what they hope and expect. The events of their lives often appear to bear no resemblance to their wants and needs, and it may be quite impossible to discern an overall purpose from the occurrence of those events.

This is also true of the church. Although it is asserted in Scripture that the church is the bride of Christ, redeemed by his blood, and the object of the special care and love of God, nevertheless the Christian church has often been subjected to terrible persecution in which God appears not to care. From time to time she has been led by foolish and corrupt men. She has suffered internal dissension, fratricide, megalomania; she has been riven by doctrinal disputes. Far from the blood of the martyrs always being the seed of the church, their blood has often heralded the eclipse of the church from parts of the earth. How can all these occurrences be reconciled with the claim that God cares and provides for the church?

It is also true of the universe at large. How can the providential care of God over his creation be reconciled with disease, decay and death; with war and famine; and with human viciousness and faithlessness? How can it be reconciled with physical calamities, earthquakes, violent storms and viruses?

These are acute problems, much discussed but little understood and resolved. Within the scope of a work such as this, it is impossible to encompass the vast amount of discussion that there has been on the problem of evil and the various strategies by which people have sought to justify the ways of God. An attempt will be made to say something about these questions later in the book, in the light of the doctrine of divine providence outlined in the earlier chapters. In the context of a discussion of divine providence, these difficult questions seem to raise two kinds of problem.

There are, first, problems to do with knowledge and belief. Given a prior belief in God's providence, derived from the Scriptures, how are we to know that God is guiding us in a particular direction? How are we to decide what to do? Indeed, does the character of our decision change at all, given our belief in providence? Would our attitude be any different if we believed that God did not 'provide', but instead ran a cosmic lottery? These questions are often of acute concern to people facing particular choices of career, for example, or trying to assess priorities between different courses of action. What part should the knowledge that God is active now play in such reasoning processes?

There are also moral issues of a particularly acute kind. The problem of evil is often presented as a problem of consistency: how can the existence of an omnipotent, all-good God be consistent with the existence of moral evil and physical calamity? This is indeed a problem. But in the context of a treatment of divine providence this problem is faced in a more acute form. This is because divine providence, at least as we shall understand it, focuses upon omnipotence as exercised in the direct *control* of the creation. So the problem is not merely 'How can God permit or allow evil?' but 'How can there be evil in a universe which God controls?'

The 'problem of evil' often surfaces in a distinctive way during discussions about providence. Suppose someone falls down a flight of stairs but escapes serious injury. It may be said that such an escape was providential, a verdict which would gain wide acceptance among Christians. But what about the fall itself? Was that providential as well?

The point can be generalized. If (let us say) God is alleged to have providentially intervened at Dunkirk, then why did he not providentially intervene more often? Why was there not intervention at Belsen or Auschwitz? Why, in general, are there not *more* interventions? In a later chapter it will be necessary to discuss these darker questions, and also the whole idea of providence as 'intervention', in more detail.

An agenda of problems

Taking our cue from our survey of these problems, we may summarize our agenda for studying the Christian doctrine of divine providence in a rather different way. That doctrine, as it applies to any one of the three separate contexts of interest that we have identified, raises three sorts of problem which have to be satisfactorily resolved if the doctrine is to be coherent and credible.

The first of these is the problem of the relation of God's existence and activity to the existence and activity of his creatures, particularly human beings. How is it possible to preserve the activity of each and not to lapse into either pantheism (according to which God is identical with the universe) or deism (according to which he is wholly separate from it and unconcerned with it now)?

The second set of problems has to do with our knowledge. Granted that God provides, is it possible to know, in any particular instance, that God has guided, or that he is guiding, or that he will guide? What operational difference does either the fact of God's providence, or the belief that God is providing, make in the life of a person?

The final item on our agenda is to discuss the moral problems that the idea of providence raises. How can the moral character of God as wholly good be preserved in the face of the fact that he controls even the most vicious actions of his creatures? How can we escape the cynical view that, in governing all his creatures and their actions, God allows the end to justify the means? Further, how can we continue to assert human responsibility and accountability in the face of such control?

Some observations on method

In providing this preliminary orientation it has been repeatedly stated that we are attempting to set forth a *Christian* doctrine of divine providence. What does this mean, and what does it imply in terms of method?

It means in the first place that the data from which the doctrine is constructed will be drawn from Scripture, or interpreted as far as possible in the light of its teaching. In the history of western thought there have been attempts to derive a doctrine of divine providence from reason alone. One notable instance is the argument of Gottfried von Leibniz (1646–1716) that this, the actual world, is the best of all possible worlds. Another case occurs as part of the argument for God's existence known as the 'argument from design'. According to this argument the universe shows clear signs of the existence of a powerful and benevolent creator, and part of that evidence arises from the order and coherence of the universe.

The important question for us is not whether these attempts succeed in establishing the Christian doctrine of divine providence, but whether they adopt the appropriate method in making the attempt. In what follows it will be assumed that they do not, but rather that the materials for the construction of all that is distinctive of such a doctrine are to be found only in God's special revelation. The extent to which, when that doctrine is established, we may also expect to find confirmation of it from general features of the universe, is a matter for further debate.

The materials will thus, as far as possible, be drawn from Scripture. But of course the Bible is not a ready-made book of Christian doctrine, with a convenient chapter on providence. The word 'providence' does not appear in Scripture. The data in terms of which an account of God's providence is to be constructed are scattered throughout the books of Scripture in a variety of settings. This reminds us that the 'providence of God' is not a theoretical concept, but refers to the activity of God in the individual lives of men and women. Our aim, therefore, must be to draw together the threads of these data into a balanced and consistent whole.

Sometimes a contrast is drawn between an 'inductive' and a 'deductive' approach to the data of Scripture, usually for the purpose of applauding the inductive approach and deploring the deductive. The contrast is, however, a false one. In any treatment of the biblical data there must be

27

elements of each. There must, to begin with, be some general view about divine providence drawn deductively from some of the data. But because our grasp of the data is only partial, even valid deductions may not convey a rounded doctrine. So there is need to treat the first derivations of the doctrine with appropriate caution, and to return to the data, in the belief that the original idea may be suitably modified and refined in the process. An initial deduction must be followed by fresh inductions, and these in turn followed by revised deductions, until there is a reasonable belief that all the relevant data have been covered.

In this process human reason (yours and mine) necessarily plays a part. This is a risky business, of course, but in the circumstances it is plainly unavoidable. The call that is sometimes heard for a 'purely biblical' account of a doctrine, an account that is quite unconnected and unaffected by human reason, is an impossibility. What could such a biblical doctrine be? Even a mere recitation of biblical texts involves human reason in the selection of the texts, in deciding which texts are relevant and which are not.

The way that our reasoning must operate in articulating the data derived from Scripture is as follows. It is an axiom of the Christian faith that Scripture is self-consistent. And so it follows that *prima facie* contradictions or inconsistencies among the data must be capable of resolution. It is the place of reason to assist in that resolution while allowing, as with any intellectual enquiry, the existence at any one time of unresolved knots and anomalies. Having derived the data from Scripture in as consistent a form as possible, it is also the place of reason to deduce from those data whatever is judged to follow from them, and to draw out the implications of the resultant doctrine for other Christian doctrines.

The challenge for human reason is to avoid imposing a doctrine upon the data in an *a priori* fashion, muffling and silencing the testimony of Scripture by deciding, in advance, what Scripture must and must not say. This is the stratagem of every rationalist and it must be avoided at all costs. How can it be avoided? Not by silencing rational reflection altogether, but by controlling it. But how?

It has been said that sometimes Christian theologians have

attempted to derive Christian doctrine by deduction from
one axiom. This is especially relevant in connection with
divine providence. It has been specifically alleged that certain
Christian theologians in the past have used the idea of predestination as the sole theological axiom, deriving all else
from it. A moment's reflection, however, will be enough to
show that this must be a nonsense. For how could, say, the
death of Christ, or the proposition 'Christ died for our sins',
be deduced from the idea of God's providence? Whether or
not Christ died for our sins depends solely upon whether or
not Christ's death occurred, whether it was part of God's
providence. We can discover this only by examining the relevant data.

But a different sort of proposal may be made, not that
divine providence or predestination is the axiom from which
all the remainder of Christian theology derives, but that it is
possible to derive the doctrine of providence from the concept of God alone. That is, having established the doctrine of
God from Scripture, it may be argued that the doctrine of
providence follows as a matter of logic; it can be 'read off'
from the divine character. In his treatment of providence the
Protestant Reformer Zwingli (1484–1531) appears to have
attempted something of this sort.[2]

Such a procedure is not altogether unreasonable. From the
fact that God is the Creator of the universe, that he is holy,
all-knowing and all-powerful, and that he has purposes or
ends which he brings to pass, much can be deduced about the
fact that he sustains and controls his creation. But it would be
a mistake to think that the whole of the nature of divine
providence can be derived in this way.

For one thing, could the *extent* of God's providence
(whether, for example, it extends not only to the outward
actions of his creatures but also to their thoughts) be deduced
from the character of God alone? Perhaps it could. Bearing
in mind our three contexts, however, it is certainly impossible
to derive from the character of God alone the fact that he has
a church and that he cares for her. These data can be derived
only from his special revelation in Scripture. /

The way forward, therefore, is to allow the data of Scripture to control the whole of our understanding of divine

providence by using it to reflect upon preliminary conclusions to which our earlier review of the data led. We start with some rough and preliminary idea of divine providence, and attempt to refine this successively by allowing the data of Scripture (in its full range and variety) to modify it. Such a preliminary idea has, in effect, already been provided in the orientation in this chapter. The chapters which follow are an attempt to refine this further.

When we have refined our preliminary view of divine providence in the light of the scriptural data as much as it is possible to do, what exactly will we have achieved? It is important to stress here what is, and what is not, being claimed for such a doctrinal statement. What results is a *model* or a partial model, of God's relationship to his creation, not a *theory*. The distinction is an important one, and so requires explanation.

In the natural sciences, a good theory explains the occurrence of certain data, doing so in a simple and economical way, and enabling predictions of the future occurrence of more such data to be made. Such explanations provide understanding, and on the basis of that understanding enable the scientist, in a measure, to control the future. But this is not what happens in the formulation of a Christian doctrine.

To begin with, though we are dealing with complex sets of data, those data are not naturally occurring, nor are they repeatable under experimental conditions. The data are given as a result of a divine revelation; otherwise they are not known. Furthermore, the data, in so far as they concern the relationship between God and one or other aspect of his creation, are without precedent and without parallel in human experience.

Theological doctrines cannot be scientific explanations because, unlike science, it is impossible to appeal to any laws which render them intelligible and enable future events to be predicted. What might seem more promising is if they could be seen as personal explanations, like certain kinds of explanation in history and in the social sciences – explanations in terms of the reason and intention of the agent. God is, after all, supremely personal. But further reflection will show that this cannot be the case. It is impossible to render the data intelligible by invoking God's intentions, since the only way of understanding God's intentions lies through the data which he has chosen to reveal. It is not as if it is possible to have a separate and direct access to the mind of God in order to explain and make intelligible what he is doing and telling us in Scripture. The only access we have to the mind of God is through what he has revealed about (among other things) his providential rule.

So if theological doctrines are not scientific explanations, and not personal explanations, what are they? I suggest that they are not explanations of any kind. They are *models*, which have at least a twofold function. One of these functions has already been mentioned: that of drawing together the relevant data in as consistent and coherent a fashion as possible. Part of the aim in such statements of doctrine is to be as *exact* as possible. An exact statement is one that requires the minimal amount of further qualification. The exactness is not that of scientific theory but the exactness of summary.

An example of such exactness is the statement of the Westminster Shorter Catechism in answer to the question, 'What are God's works of providence?'

> God's works of providence are, his most holy, wise, and powerful preserving and governing all his creatures, and all their actions.

This is offered, in the Catechism, as an exact statement of the doctrine. It aims to summarize the teaching of Scripture in as precise a fashion as possible, using language that calls for as little qualification as possible. The use of similes and metaphors and figures of speech is minimized. It is perfectly clear, however, that this statement is not a theory. Someone who believes that the statement of the Catechism is true is not able to explain anything that could not be explained before. Possibly he is able to ascribe things to God that he could not ascribe before, but such ascription does not function as an explanation. Indeed, it might be said that it renders the need for explanations all the more necessary.

The second function that such statements perform is to

prevent or discourage false inferences being drawn from the data which they summarize.

Because they deal with matters which are without precedent or parallel in human experience, theological statements have great potential for misunderstanding. It is only too easy to draw false inferences from them (or from parts of them), hence the need to take due account of the statements as a whole. To illustrate this further, we turn again to the Shorter Catechism which contains the following claims: that God preserves and governs all his creatures; that his preserving and governing of them extends to all their actions; and that his preserving and governing of them is most holy, wise and powerful. Among the inferences that this formulation is designed to prevent, then, are the following:

– that God preserves and governs only some of his creatures;

– that God preserves and governs only some of the actions of his creatures;

– that God's preserving and governing of his creatures is weak or inept;

– that God's holiness is compromised by his preserving and governing of any actions of his creatures;

– that in the governing and preserving of his creatures God desires certain ends that he is not powerful enough to effect.

There are, obviously, other inferences which are not clearly included in or excluded from the statement; for example:

– that in governing and preserving his creatures God governs their thoughts and desires.

– that in governing and preserving his creatures God acts through intermediaries.

It could be argued that actions do not include thoughts; or it might be counter-argued, 'How could God govern all his creatures and all their actions without governing their thoughts?' If God governs and preserves his creatures through intermediaries, does he govern and preserve the intermediaries in precisely the same way?

But what is patent is that the statement drawn from the Catechism makes no attempt to answer theoretical questions. What is notably absent from it is any attempt to explain *how*

God is able to effect his works of providence. And because the governor is not another creature, we can be sure that any attempts to explain this relationship in terms of one or other of the ways in which one creature may govern another will necessarily fail.

Some of the ways in which one creature governs another are by enforceable laws, by threats, by electrical currents, by strings, by financial incentives, by sexual favours, by example, or by praise. It would be quite wrong to conclude that, because God is said to govern his creatures and their actions, he therefore governs them by any of the ways in which one creature may govern another. Perhaps there are occasions when God does so, but it would be unwarranted to conclude that his governing does and must always take this form. These considerations will be of the utmost importance when we study, later on, the question of the harmony between the divine governing of his creatures and their own personal responsibility and accountability. It may be that whenever one creature governs another, the one governed suffers a diminution of his personal responsibility. Even if this is true, it does not follow that when God governs his creatures they are not responsible for what they do.

So, to summarize, the function of doctrinal statements is twofold – to encapsulate the scriptural data in summary form, and in such a form as to block off unwarranted inferences. Their function is not to provide explanations of what cannot, because of its unparalled character, be explained to us.

In considering any aspect of God's relation to the universe, then, we are dealing with situations which are without parallel and which we cannot directly experience. This means that, unlike our enquires into the natural sciences, the resulting doctrine is not capable of answering our 'How?' questions. It is readily granted that from an intellectual point of view this situation is not the ideal, but then, in this area, as in all other areas of human enquiry, it behoves enquirers to be responsive to the character of the data, and not to impose their own ideas upon them. Untold damage has been done in the Christian church by a failure to observe these intellectual limits.

There are also intellectual limits of a different kind. In

considering divine providence we are dealing with the activity of one who is the supremely personal creator and Lord of the universe. The doctrine of providence enables us to say, of any event or action in the universe, that God either brought it to pass, or, at the very least, permitted it as part of his providential control of the whole. But what it is impossible for us to do is to provide an intellectually satisfying answer to the 'Why?' question. For asking such a question can only call forth the answer, 'Because God willed it to be so.' To the subsequent question, 'Why did God will it to be so?' there is no further, illuminating answer. This is one reason that the pattern of divine providence will, in this life at least, always be a mystery.

In dealing with the providence of God, therefore, we are dealing with matters of ultimate significance for which there is no further explanation. This does not mean that God is arbitrary or capricious in his dealings with the created universe. What it does mean is that the will of God, and the holy and wise reasons that he has for the exercise of that will, are the highest court of appeal (highest in the logical sense). There cannot be a higher court, and so, unsatisfactory though it may be, we must rest content with that ultimate reference to the will of God.

Scepticism about God's action

Most of this chapter has been spent setting out an agenda of problems, and with formulating an appropriate method of investigation. But it is easy to anticipate the objection that this begs one important question. Our discussion so far, preliminary though it has been, assumes that it makes good sense to talk about the action or activity of God. Many philosophers and theologians, however, have questioned this. They have said, for example, that actions take time; how then can a God who exists in a timeless eternity, act?[3] It is also said that an action is necessarily performed by an *embodied* agent; but God exists in an unembodied state. How then can he be said to perform any action?

It is important to keep separate two distinct questions. One type of question is, 'how can we know, or be sure, or even

34

have the opinion, that some particular event (say the Dunkirk crossing) is an act of God?' Let us call this the problem of *identification*. This sort of question can be answered only by the accumulation of evidence of the appropriate kind. In this respect, deciding whether or not an event constituted an act of God is no different in principle from deciding that a particular event was an action of Napoleon. It is necessary to enquire into the circumstances. We hope to address this sort of question, in various guises, as we proceed with our enquiry.

There is, however, another, more basic kind of question: how does anything at all count as an act of God? This is a conceptual question; let us call it the problem of *identity*. It concerns the very idea of a divine action and it is more basic because, until the answer to this question is settled, it is not possible to address questions about identification.

Here is one contemporary expression of scepticism about the very idea of divine action:

> When God was said to have 'acted', it was believed that he had performed an observable act in space and time so that he functioned as does any secondary cause; and when he was said to have 'spoken', it was believed that an audible voice was heard by the person addressed. In other words, the words 'act' and 'speak' were used in the same sense of God as of men. We deny this univocal under-standing of theological words. To us, theological verbs such as 'to act', 'to work', 'to do', 'to speak', 'to reveal', etc., have no longer the literal meaning of observable actions in space and time or of voices in the air ... Unless one knows in some sense what the analogy means, how the analogy is being used, and what it points to, an analogy is empty and unin-telligible.[4]

Thus Langdon Gilkey, and many others, argue that God cannot be said to act in the same sense in which you or I act, and that there is no clear alternative sense. What is to be said to this?

In the first place there seem to be no grounds for Gilkey's anxieties about observability. Actions, typically, consist of unobservable causes and observable effects. A person decides to do something and then, provided that he is not impeded, he does it. Why should this not apply in the case of God? His 'willing' is hidden from us, unobserved and unobservable. But then so is your 'willing' hidden from me, and mine from you. The effects of God's 'willing' may, for all we have heard to the contrary, be public and observable; the material creation and all that it contains, and even, in the case of miracles, particular events within that creation. Why not? But some of the effects of God's actions may be unobservable, just as some human actions (such as sequences of reasoning, or of other streams of consciousness) are unobservable. Observability or otherwise does not seem to have very much to do with the concept of an action.

It might be said, however, that since we learn what an action is from seeing other people behave, 'action' cannot mean the same when applied to God as it does when applied to Mr Smith. When God allegedly speaks, for example, vocal cords have nothing to do with it. This is a serious objection only if a reference to the vocal cords is part of the *meaning* of 'speaks'. But is it? Perhaps the meaning of 'speaks' is to be found not by reference to the body but by the bringing about of certain effects, by effecting communication.

Even if this is not so – even if the meaning of 'speaks', when used of either God or man, is not the same – why cannot the meaning as learned in the context of human speech be adapted for use in the case of divine speech? If 'speak' means 'communicate by means of the use of vocal cords', why, in the case of God, cannot 'speak' simply mean 'communicate'? As William Alston puts it:

> Even if the meanings of human action terms are
> infected with elements that prevent them from
> being applied to God, simply shear off those ele-
> ments and see what is left. It may be, and often is,
> that what is left is something that can be intelligibly
> applied to God, and in the application of which we

36

succeed in saying what we set out to say when we talk about God's action.[5]

There is, therefore, no *a priori* reason which should lead us to conclude that God cannot act, and that for that reason the very idea of divine providence is incoherent.

2

PROVIDENCE:
RISKY OR RISK-FREE?

Before we look at divine providence in more detail there is
one major matter that has to be settled. This is the question
whether, according to Scripture, divine providence is a risky
or risk-free matter; risky or risk-free for God, that is. This is a
difference of view between Christians which runs very deep;
it is at the heart of the conflict between Augustine and Pel-
agius, and also at the heart of the Reformation conflict. This
being so, there is little hope of settling the matter to everyone's satisfaction in one short chapter! Nevertheless, little
progress can be made in understanding divine providence
until we have reviewed some of the arguments on either side,
and have decided how we are to proceed in the light of this
basic division. It is the purpose of this chapter to do this.

Does God's providence, according to Scripture, extend to
all that he has created, including the choices of men and
women? Or is his providence limited, perhaps limited by God
himself, so that he does not infallibly know how the universe
is going to unfold? Let us call the first of these views (it is in
fact a family of views) the 'risk-free' or 'no-risk' view of
providence, and the second family, the 'risky' view.[1] Our

question then is: which view of providence does Scripture favour?

It is clear that there are different kinds of risk. For example, if we start something, not knowing how it will turn out, and if how it turns out matters to us then we take a risk. A risk of another, perhaps lesser, kind is where we have no formulated or expressed preference as to how we want things to turn out, but only expectations; and we set in motion events which may lead only to the partial fulfilment of our expectations, or to their non-fulfilment. In what follows we shall use 'risk' in the stronger of these senses, where both preferences and expectations are at stake. We take no risk if we knowingly set in motion events which will turn out exactly as we want them to do.

In the case of divine providence the events in question are all those which, in the history of the entire universe, are to become actual. We shall assume that if at least one of these events could be caused to turn out in a way other than the way that God believes that it will, then God is taking a risk. The risk may not be very great, and its inherent riskiness may be softened by remembering that even if God does not infallibly determine what will happen in this particular case, his control of what will happen will be considerable. Nevertheless, a risk is a risk.

It will be noted that we have formulated riskiness and risk-freeness in terms of God's *knowledge*.[2] It is also possible to formulate it in terms of God's decreeing or ordaining, and it might be thought that such a formulation would be more in accord with divine providence. If God takes a risk, however, where this is understood in terms of knowledge, then it would follow logically that he also takes a risk in terms of what he ordains. For what he ordains must be similarly risky.

Numerous contemporary theologians and philosophers take the view that God's providence must be a risky affair. Here are some representative statements:

> It is evident that the view of God's governance of the world here proposed differs from others that are commonly held. But wherein precisely does the difference lie? I believe it can be formulated in a

simple, yet crucial question: *Does God take risks?* Or, to put the matter more precisely, we may ask: *Does God make decisions that depend for their outcomes on the responses of free creatures in which the decisions themselves are not informed by knowledge of the outcomes?* If he does, then creating and governing a world is for God a risky business. That this is so is evidently an implication of the views here adopted, and it is equally evident that it would be rejected by some Christian thinkers – those, for example, who hold to a theory of predestination according to which everything that occurs is determined solely by God's sovereign decree.[3]

The value that regards knowledge as a good can be more fully realised by forgoing the possibility of being a complete know-all, and creating a world in which the future actions of others can often only be surmised, and sometimes not even that. If God created man in His own image, He must have created him capable of new initiatives and new insights which cannot be precisely or infallibly foreknown, but which give to the future a perpetual freshness as the inexhaustible variety of possible thoughts and actions, on the part of His children as well as Himself, crystallizes into actuality.[4]

... God must take real risks if He makes free creatures (thousands, millions, or trillions of risks, if each creature makes thousands of morally significant free choices). No matter how shrewdly God acted in running so many risks, His winning on *every* risk would not be antecedently probable.[5]

That God is omniscient only in the attenuated sense would of course – given that he is perfectly free and omnipotent – have resulted from his own choice. In choosing to preserve his own freedom (and to give others freedom), he limits his own knowledge of what is to come. He continually limits himself in this ways by not curtailing his or men's future freedom.

41

> As regards men, their choices are much influenced by circumstances and this makes it possible for a being who knows all the circumstances to predict human behaviour correctly most of the time, but always with the possibility that men may falsify those predictions.[6]

The following are some representative statements of the no-risk view of providence:

> Even though it may seem to us that all things happen equally to the good and to the evil since we are ignorant of the reasons for God's providence in allotting these things, there is no doubt that in all these good and evil things happening to the good or to the evil there is operative a well worked out plan by which God's providence directs all things.[7]

> But God protects and governs by His providence all things which He created, 'teaching from end to end mightily and ordering all things sweetly' (Wisdom 8:1). For 'all things are naked and open to his eyes' (Heb. 4:13), even those which by the free action of creatures are in the future.[8]

> God, the great Creator of all things, doth uphold, direct, dispose, and govern all creatures, actions and things, from the greatest even to the least, by his most wise and holy providence, according to his infallible foreknowledge, and the free and immutable counsel of his own will, to the praise of the glory of his wisdom, power, justice, goodness, and mercy.[9]

It will be noted from this selection of views on providence that the chief (if not the only) reason why a 'risk' view of providence is taken is a concern to preserve human freedom, and (in the case of Swinburne at least) to preserve divine freedom as well. All the writers hold the view that only if providence is risky will there be room for the exercise of human freedom.

'Freedom' is a term that has many meanings, and so it is important to understand what is the sense of human freedom that these writers believe it is essential to safeguard. One way of explaining this sense is as follows. If we are free, then we have the power to do some particular action, or to refrain from doing it, even though the entire history of the universe up to the moment of that choice is the same whichever choice is made. The entire history of the universe, up to the point of our choice, is consistent either with our performing of that action or with our refraining from it. So which action is performed is up to us, to the exercise of our free choice. An alternative way of expressing this, though not a strictly equivalent way, is to say that we are free in doing an action only if, every circumstance other than our decision remaining the same, we could have decided otherwise.

This is a sense of freedom which is incompatible with determinism. Only if freedom in this sense is maintained (writers such as Lucas and Swinburne believe) can justice be done to human dignity and creativity, and to human responsibility.

In later chapters, when dealing with different models of providence, and with the vexed issue of providence and evil, we shall consider in more detail the issue of human freedom, and particularly whether this view of freedom is necessary in order to uphold human dignity and responsibility., At this stage we shall consider what the consequences are for the idea of divine providence of taking a non-deterministic view of human freedom (or, more accurately, what consequences the writers just quoted are prepared to accept). These consequences have chiefly to do with God's character – his knowledge, his will and his goodness, including the character of God's saving grace. This latter point, though, is not something that looms large in current discussion. We shall briefly comment on each of these in turn.

The character of God

1. God's knowledge

As traditionally understood, God is omniscient. This is not only a consequence of the perfection of God in the abstract (for how could a perfect God be ignorant of anything?), but also of attending to the relevant data of Scripture. In Scripture God is said to be one who knows the end from the beginning; all things are naked and open before his eyes; he has numbered the hairs of our heads; he knows our downsitting and uprising, he understands our ways afar off; he knows what we need before we ask; he ordains all things after the counsel of his own will, and so on.

But if in fact God has created a universe in which there is risk, then he cannot be omniscient. Most writers who take the 'risk' view accept this. They are prepared, as a consequence, to sacrifice or to attenuate the classical and scriptural doctrine of divine omniscience in the interests of a risky providence. There are several different arguments by which such attentuation is defended, but in order to simplify and focus our discussion I shall concentrate upon one of these: that provided by Richard Swinburne in *The Coherence of Theism*.

Swinburne develops his account out of a concern not only for the preservation of human freedom, but for divine freedom. Because of his concern to safeguard freedom, Swinburne proposes the following restricted definition of omniscence:

> A person P is omniscient at a time t if and only if he knows of every true proposition about t or an earlier time that it is true *and* also he knows of every true proposition about a time later than t, such that what it reports is physically necessitated by some cause at t or earlier, that it is true.[10]

This definition may require a little explanation. Note in the first place that what is proposed is a general definition of omniscience, one that could apply not only to God but to any

44

person. Also, whoever it applies to is in time, for the definition refers to ominscience *at a time*. If God is timelessly eternal, as some have argued, then this definition could not apply to him. Perhaps, though, it could be suitably modified.

The basic thought behind the definition, however, is that an omniscient being knows everything about the past and about the present, and he also knows whatever is 'physically necessitated' by any cause in the present or past. Such an omniscient being would know, for example, that I am typing these sentences on my wordprocessor now, and he would also know what the movements of the planets will be tomorrow, and what the state of any remote forest, physically inaccessible to human interference, will be tomorrow. What he will not know today is anything whatever about tomorrow which depends upon non-physically necessitated choices, particularly human decisions. Thus, if I have not yet made up my mind whether or not, by a free action, to chop down my cherry tree tomorrow, then God cannot yet know what the state of that tree will be tomorrow. He would of course otherwise know what its state tomorrow will be, since its state tomorrow (freely decided-upon interference apart) is physically necessitated by its state today.

Swinburne stresses the importance for limiting omniscience of what is not *physically* necessitated, but this restriction may not cover all the cases that he has in mind. For some have argued, not that human choices are physically necessitated, but that they are psychologically necessitated or even rationally necessitated. That is, they have claimed that human choices are the outcome not of prior physical states, but of prior psychological states such as desires, wishes and preferences of various kinds. Still, Swinburne's account can be modified to cover such cases, simply by dropping the word 'physical' from it.

In saying that God (for example) does not *know* what a person (including himself) will freely choose tomorrow, Swinburne is not denying that God may have *beliefs* about the future.

> In choosing to preserve his own freedom (and to give others freedom), he (that is, God) limits his own

knowledge of what is to come. He continually limits himself in this way by not curtailing his or men's future freedom. As regards men, their choices are much influenced by circumstances and this makes it possible for a being who knows all the circumstances to predict human behaviour correctly most of the time, but always with the possibility that men may falsify those predictions.[11]

Knowing what he does about the present and the past, God may (as we noted earlier) have very accurate beliefs. Nonetheless these beliefs do not amount to knowledge. God has beliefs (we may presume), many of which turn out to be false as, due to the free decisions of men and women, what he supposes will happen does not in fact happen. Not only, therefore, is God's omniscience restricted in the way indicated, but his infallibility must also be surrendered. We shall return to this point later.

Such an account of omniscience differs markedly from that given by the great theologians of Christianity. For example:

> Now, if the infinity of numbers cannot be beyond the limits of the knowledge of God which comprehends it, who are we little men that we should presume to put limits to His knowledge? ... The fact is that God, whose knowledge is simple in its multiplicity and one in its diversity, comprehends all incomprehensible things with an incomprehensible comprehension.[12]

> Whatever can be produced or thought or said by a creature, and also whatever God himself can produce, all is known by God, even if it is not actually existing.[13]

> Concerning repentance, we ought so to hold that it is no more chargeable against God than is ignorance.[14]

46

While Swinburne acknowledges that his account of omniscience is less strict than that usually attributed to God by Christian theologians, he nevertheless claims scriptural support for it. He cites, for example, the fact that in the Old Testament God has certain plans which he on occasion changes. He changed his plan regarding Sodom when Abraham interceded, and spared Israel when Moses interceded; he spared Nineveh when Jonah preached, and so on. In general, Swinburne says, God would not need to make conditional promises if he knew what men would do.

> By contrast, the New Testament talks a great deal of God's 'foreknowledge', but, at any rate sometimes, it does not seem to regard this as absolute. Man can upset God's plans.[15]

So there are, in effect, two types of scriptural data. One type indicates that God's knowledge is unqualified. The other type of data represents God as learning, as forgetting, as changing his mind, as being surprised, and the like. What, then, ought we to conclude? What part do such data play in an account of divine providence which is not only coherent in itself but in accordance with all the data of Scripture? We shall consider an answer to this question shortly.

2. God's will

There are several senses in which God is said to have a will. God may will in the sense of *command*, and he may will in the sense of *decree*. My cherry tree exists by God's decree, but God has not commanded the tree to exist. (We might say that he has commanded that the tree exist, but not that he has commanded it *to* exist.) After all, it is possible to issue commands only to what already exists, and until God has commanded that the tree exist there is no tree for him to issue commands to.

It is not easy to suppose that God might issue commands to trees. But according to Scripture, from time to time he has commanded men and women. Sometimes these commands have to do with particular people, times and places; sometimes they are more general, even universal, in their

47

scope. God's command to Abraham to sacrifice Issac was specific. His command forbidding stealing was issued to Israel, and perhaps applies more widely still.

Not every command of God is obeyed. Scripture teaches, however, that even on those occasions when the command of God is disobeyed, the disobedience is in accordance with his will, in the sense of his decree. Scripture is littered with examples of such cases. It was against the command of God (presumably) that Joseph's brothers should sell him, but in this way God decreed a saviour for Israel. Through Saul's disobedience David became king. Again, through the murderous intentions of the Jews and the weakness of Pilate, Jesus was crucified.

Perhaps these events could have been brought about without violations of God's command. We shall not speculate on this. It is sufficient to note that *in fact* they did not come about in such ways, but what God decreed involved violations of commands that he himself had given. To put the point paradoxically, the breaking of his will became part of the fulfilling of his will. We shall consider the character of God's will in more detail in chapter 5.

If, however, one supposes a 'risk' view of providence, this picture appears to change in a radical way. According to some Christian theologians who support such a view, there are at least some significant occasions which contain elements undecreed by God, or on which, though God has decreed a certain definite outcome, that decree is thwarted or modified by the exercise of human libertarian free will. While, on this view God *unconditionally* decrees much (for example, those aspects of his creation never affected by libertarian choices), he also *conditionally* decrees much, thereby taking risks. Similarly, just as his commands (for instance, not to steal) may be broken, so may what he has decreed, if what he has decreed falls foul of free choice. Those who make such a choice may not know that they are thwarting God's decree (for that decree may not have been disclosed to anyone), but this does not alter the fact of the matter.

In fact, however, the matter runs deeper than this. On the 'risk' view of divine providence, not only may a free decision thwart the decree of God, but God's decreeing any human action is inconsistent with that action's being indeterministically free. For, as we have seen, the essence of indeterministic freedom is a power to choose either A or not – A in a situation where the character of the universe, up to the moment of the choice, is fixed. So what God may or may not have decreed about the choice, prior to its exercise, is *irrelevant* to the exercise of such a choice.

Various ways have been proposed to mitigate the effects of this collision between God's decree and human libertarian freedom, to minimize or eliminate the risk. It has been proposed, for example, that we should think of the relation of God to his free creatures as like that of a chess Grand Master, who is able effortlessly to outwit the freely made chess moves of any number of novices.[16] Perhaps the most influential proposal for avoiding the collision is the doctrine of God's middle knowledge. We shall consider this possibility later in the chapter.

3. God's goodness

The question whether or not providence is risky also affects the character of God's goodness.

God's goodness may be considered from various aspects, and in almost all these aspects it is a bone of contention. Chief controversial interest is at present focused on the extensiveness of God's goodness. Granted that many men and women lead tolerable and personally fulfilling lives, why does God not bring it about that everyone does? Why are God's blessings uneven? Why is there discrimination? Why do the wicked prosper? If God is good, and all-powerful, why has he not arranged matters so as to minimize suffering and to maximize individual pleasure? These questions form the heart of the problem of evil, and we shall look at this in greater detail in chapter 8.

There is, however, another way in which the goodness of God may be considered which is less frequently debated at present. We might call this the *intensiveness* question. Given that God wishes to do good, how effective can these wishes be? Can he wish to do good to a person and be thwarted by that person? In other words, in carrying out his plans to do good, does God take risks?

49

Historically, this question has been at the centre of a controversy about divine saving grace. Is that grace merely *enabling*, or is it *effective*? How that question is answered will vitally affect the providence of God as it concerns the existence and character of the Christian church. Is the church formed as a result of men and women taking advantage of certain favourable conditions and circumstances provided by God in his goodness? Or does God's goodness actually cause the church to be formed by bringing about the conversion of men and women to Christ?

In Scripture God's grace in conversion is powerful (1 Thes. 1:5); it is an effective call (Rom. 1:6; 9:11; 1 Cor. 1:9; Eph. 4:4); it is compared to a creation (2 Cor. 4:6), and to resurrection (Eph. 2:5), and to a new birth (1 Pet. 1:23). The Holy Spirit gives repentance (2 Tim. 2:25) and faith (Eph. 2:8). Both the plain and the figurative language used about conversion seems to point unmistakably to the idea that God's grace is effective in securing the ends at which it aimed.

It is hard to see how one can hold both (a) that God's goodness is effective in the way that these verses describe (*i.e.* that it is causally sufficient for making a person a Christian) and (b) that people have indeterministic freedom to choose whether or not to be converted. It would certainly be possible to hold that there are many indeterministic choices but that Christian conversion does not include any, though this is not a view that is readily found in the history of Christian thought. If, at the point of conversion, we have indeterministic power, then we have indeterministic power to reject the efforts of God's goodness to bring about our conversion. It would then follow that in offering his goodness in these circumstances God was taking a risk.

Yet what is one to make of the scriptural references to men and women resisting the grace of God (Acts 7:51) and rejecting the message of salvation (Acts 13:46)? Is Scripture simply contradictory at this point, or 'paradoxical'? Can the data be combined together consistently by taking certain expressions to have priority over others? It is here that we need to return to the point raised earlier in the discussion of Swinburne's position.

Accommodation

We are faced with apparently incompatible data – data which on the one hand stress God's omniscience and the power of his grace, and on the other portray him as changing his mind, and men and women resisting his grace. How then is one to proceed in constructing from Scripture an account of divine omniscience or goodness, and with it an account of divine providence? Which of these apparently inconsistent or incompatible sets of data is to take priority? Which data control the remainder?

One alternative would be to say that the language about God's ignorance, about his changes of mind and resistance to his grace, is more basic to our understanding of God than the more general statements (quoted earlier) about the extent of God's knowledge or the efficacy of his grace. Statements which imply God's ignorance and powerlessness thus take precedence over statements which do not. As a consequence, we should be committed to maintaining that God is at times ignorant, that he changes his mind, that he is open to persuasion, that his purposes of goodness are thwarted, and so on. Not only this; but by parity of reasoning from the language of Scripture about God, we should also be committed to the view that God has a rich, ever-changing emotional life, and perhaps that he has a body, and a physical location in heaven.

As a consequence of accepting this principle of biblical interpretation, the scriptural language which ascribes omniscience or gracious power to God would be understood as hyperbolic; to ascribe omniscience to God is exactly like ascribing it to a human expert, to someone who knows everything about his subject. To say that God is gracious is rather like saying that a generous friend, whose gifts may be spurned, is gracious.

The alternative hermeneutical position would be to say that general scriptural statements of the omniscience, will and effective goodness of God take precedence. The other language of Scripture, the language of ignorance, of indecision and of change, is then to be interpreted in the light of these statements.

There is therefore a straight choice. Put in such a stark way it seems obvious (to me at least) what that choice ought to be. The statements about the extent and intensity of God's knowledge, power and goodness must control the anthropomorphic and weaker statements, and not vice versa. The alternative approach would appear to be quite unacceptable, for it would result in a theological reductionism in which God is distilled to human proportions.

But why, if the biblical language which portrays God as ignorant or vacillating or ultimately resistible, cannot be literally true, is it employed in Scripture? No better general answer has been given to this question, to my mind, that the one found throughout the writings of John Calvin; namely, that God uses such language to accommodate himself to human incapacity and weakness.

Accommodation, the need for God to address men and women in terms that they can understand and respond to, would seem to be a good general explanation for the occurrence of such language in Scripture, for two interconnected reasons. To begin with, it preserves the proper sense of direction. The presence of anthropomorphic language in Scripture is not a human attempt to express the inexpressible, but is one of the ways in which God graciously condescends to his creatures. As Calvin put it, referring to passages where God is said to 'repent':

> What, therefore, does the word 'repentance' mean? Surely its meaning is like that of all other modes of speaking that describe God for us in human terms. For because our weakness does not attain to his exalted state, the description of him that is given to us must be accommodated to our capacity so that we may understand it. Now the mode of accommodation is for him to represent himself to us not as he is in himself, but as he seems to us.[17]

In Calvin's eyes the movement of direction is from God to mankind, and not vice versa. Furthermore, because such language is an act of accommodation it is also an act of grace. Divine revelation is evangelical in motive and in manner, as well as in content.

But does this not reduce much of the language of Scripture to a mere teaching tool, a concession to those of weak capacity (as thinkers as different as Philo and John Locke have maintained)? While this may be our initial reaction, behind what may seem a psychological or epistemological economy on God's part, there lies a logical point of some importance.

Calvin's claim is not that human beings will not understand God at all unless he condescends to speak to us in human-like, activistic ways. For there is much in the writings of Calvin to show that he took the opposite view. The very fact that he regards certain expressions as divine *accommodations* implies that it is possible to think of God in ways which are exact and unaccommodated.

What then lies behind Calvin's view? He recognizes that it is because God wishes people to respond to him that he *must* represent himself to them as one to whom response is possible, and as one who is responsive, who acts in space and time in reaction to human actions in space and time. Only on such an understanding is it possible to provide for that divine–human interaction which is at the heart of biblical religion.

At the centre of Calvin's doctrine of divine accommodation, therefore, is a logical point: namely that it is a logically necessary condition of dialogue between people that those people should act and react in time. Omniscience and omnipotence have priority because they are essential properties of God, whereas his creating a universe in which there are creatures with whom he converses is a contingent matter. Nevertheless, if dialogue between God and mankind is to be real and not make-believe, then God cannot inform those with whom he converses of what they will decide to do, for then they would not *decide* to do it, and dialogue would be impossible.

God is portrayed in Scripture as separate from his creation, as self-sufficient, and as bringing into being a creation which is distinct from himself. On the other hand, God is also shown in anthropomorphic ways, and his action and character are also likened to non-human animals and to inanimate things. The reason for such portrayals is both pragmatic and logical: the need to represent God to human beings in ways

53

which do not (as Calvin would have put it) pander to the natural, sinful torpor and sluggishness of the human mind; and also the need for God to reveal himself in such a way as to make dialogue possible between himself and his human creatures.

Both the anthropomorphic and the exact language of Scripture are, of course, equally important, but in constructing a coherent account of God one set of data must take priority over the other. If readers believe that to give priority to the metaphysical over the apparently figurative is a mistaken decision, then it will be possible for them to make the necessary adjustments through the discussion that follows. These adjustments, however, are not small, and, if they are carried through consistently, a substantially different account of divine providence will ensue.

Costs and benefits

We are now in a position to summarize briefly our discussion so far. The costs of a 'risk' view of providence, however minimal the degree of risk is judged to be, are that God cannot be regarded as infallibly omniscient of his creation, nor is he able to bring to pass everything that he might wish to do. There will, in the life of God, necessarily be some frustration as those ends that he wishes to secure cannot be achieved, or must be achieved by a different route. God will have many true beliefs about the future; he will be highly informed and expert, but his knowledge will be like your knowledge and mine – it will be fallible. Alternatively, infallibility will be purchased at the expense of ignorance.

Similarly, it will follow that the exercise of God's redeeming grace can never, on the 'risk' view of divine providence, be efficacious. His grace is always resistible by the person on whom it operates. If it were not resistible, the action which results from such grace could not be a free action in the sense of the concept of 'freedom' being defended. For nothing that has been ensured to happen by the power of divine grace can be indeterministically free.

This would be a somewhat ironic result given the teaching of Christ that whoever the Son makes free is free indeed (Jn.

8:36). The New Testament appears to find no incoherence in the idea of being made to be free, and has little concern with the prospect that any person whose action is caused cannot be free in performing that action.

Further, as we noted briefly earlier, it appears that the 'risk' view of providence carries with it the consequence that God is in time, and so is not timelessly eternal. For a God whose knowledge and purposes are both modifiable by human, free decisions must be in time, for any such modifications must take place in time. This consequence is one that is certainly recognized and even welcomed by, for example, Swinburne and Lucas.

The benefits of the 'risk' view can be put down to the presence of one factor – an indeterministic view of free will, a view of freedom which gives an individual power, in identical circumstances, either to act or not to act, as he or she chooses.

It has often been claimed that such a view of freedom is incoherent; and of course if that were so the benefits would be lost at a stroke. I shall not claim that such a view of human freedom is incoherent, but shall continue to question, in subsequent chapters, whether such an account of freedom is necessary for human responsibility in the way in which its defenders claim.

Middle knowledge

So far, we have presented the 'risk' view of providence (resting on an indeterministic view of human freedom) and the 'no-risk' as exclusive alternatives. But they may not be. It may be possible to combine the strong view of human freedom and a 'no-risk' view of divine providence. If such a combination is possible, it would in the eyes of many represent the best of all possible outcomes; a strong view of providence and a strong, indeterministic view of human freedom.

One subtle and ambitious way of attempting to reconcile a 'no risk' view of providence with an account of human action which is indeterministic was provided by the Jesuit theologian, Luís De Molina (1535–1600). His view has recently been revived by Alvin Plantinga and has been given renewed

THE PROVIDENCE OF GOD

and intensive attention.[18] The idea of middle knowledge can briefly be explained in the following way.

How are we to understand the omniscience of God, the idea that God knows all truths? One helpful way is to pay attention to the sorts of truths that there are for God to know. There are, to begin with, *necessary truths*; for instance, the laws of logic and arithmetic. Such truths could not be false. Their truth does not depend upon God willing them to be true; he knows them to be true because he is omniscient.

Then there are the myriad truths which are true as a result of God's will. For example, London is the capital of England, and the battle of Hastings was fought in 1066. These, and all such truths, are true in virtue of the fact that God has willed them to be true. Had not God freely willed them, then they would not be true. For this reason his knowledge of them is sometimes said to be *free knowledge*. They come about as the result of God's free decision. God does not know these truths at a time after willing them, but he knows them in willing them, rather in the way in which we know many of our own actions in doing them.

Besides these two kinds of knowledge, there is also the knowledge that God has of all possibilities which he does not will, but which remain abstract possibilities. For example, Bognor Regis is the capital of England, and the battle of Hastings was fought in 1660. Among such possibilities are conditional propositions; for instance, if Bognor Regis had been capital of England, London would have fewer than one million inhabitants. Again, if John had married Joan they would have had three children. God's knowledge of such possibilities has been called *middle knowledge*; knowledge midway between God's knowledge of necessary truths, and God's free knowledge.

The Bible gives examples of God's knowledge of such possibilities. Two biblical passages became famous in the discussions: 1 Samuel 23:7–13 and Matthew 11:20–24. What the first passage makes clear is that God knew that if David were to remain in the city of Keilah, then Saul would come for him; and that if Saul were to arrive in Keilah for David, the men of Keilah would surrender David to him. What Jesus affirms in the passage from Matthew is that, if his mighty

56

works had been performed in impenitent Tyre and Sidon, they would have repented.

From these data there can be no doubt of the fact of God's middle knowledge, his knowledge of possibilities which are never brought to pass. God knew what would have happened had David remained in Keilah. But David did not remain in Keilah. Christ knew what would have happened to Tyre and Sidon had his mighty works been performed there. But the works were not performed there.

God, then, in his omniscience, knows propositions which could not be false, and propositions which could be false but which are true. He also knows propositions which could be true, but which are not in fact true, such as these concerning David and Keilah, and concerning Tyre and Sidon and Christ's mighty works. It is from this vast array of possibilities that God in his wisdom and goodness wills the actual world, the world which you and I inhabit.

It ought to be stressed that all this is common ground both to Molina and to his opponents; each side allows for the idea of middle knowledge. What is distinctive of Molina's view is that he claims that among the conditional propositions which God knows are those which indicate what would happen if an individual performed a free (*i.e.*, non-deterministic) action. He knows, that is, myriads of propositions of the form:

> (A) In circumstances C, if Jones freely chooses between X and Y, he will choose Y.

And, Molina asserts, it is because God knows all the outcomes of all the possible free choices that people will make, that he is able to create – to actualize – just those possibilities which are necessary for him to fulfil his purposes, and which involve indeterministically free choices. Hence, the free choices of creatures are compatible with God's perfect foreknowledge and his 'no-risk' providential rule of his creation. As William Lane Craig, a defender of middle knowledge, has put it:

> Since God knows what any free creature would do in any situation, he can, by creating the appropriate situations, bring it about that creatures will achieve

his ends and purposes and that they will do so *freely*.[19]

Let us see how this works out in detail by taking a trivial but concrete example. It is supposed that among the propositions that God knows are the following conditional propositions:

> (A) Only if Jones were placed in circumstances C, and were free to choose between A and B, would he choose A.

> (B) Only if Jones were placed in circumstances C*, and were free to choose between A and B, would he choose B.

Let us suppose that God wills that Jones chooses B. In that eventuality, clearly God will actualize circumstances C*.

There is one major difficulty, however, with this supposition. It is that Jones is supposed to be indeterministically free. Because he is indeterministically free, he has the power, if he is free in a given set of circumstances, to choose any one of a number of alternatives open to him. As the defenders of middle knowledge frequently put it, which of the alternatives Jones chooses is up to him, not up to God.

If this is so, then God cannot know that (A) or (B) is true. And because he cannot know that A is true he cannot actualize (A) *as a whole*. He can actualize Jones, and he can actualize circumstances C; what he cannot do is actualize Jones's freely choosing A in circumstances C. For whether or not Jones does choose A when placed in circumstances C is up to Jones.

The proponents of middle knowledge present the following seductive picture of God's relation to various conditional possibilities. It is as if God has before his mind's eye innumerable files. Each of these files is consistent and complete. Each one represents a possible segment of the universe. God surveys all the files, and selects those which, together, form that universe which, in his wisdom and goodness, he wills to bring to pass. Among the files are those which contain references to human free actions in certain circumstances. God actualizes those files which refer to circumstances which, if the individuals are placed in them, and act freely, they will choose in accordance with the end which God desires. Thus, it is said, human freedom is preserved, and the 'no-risk' view of providence is also preserved.

The strength of the middle-knowledge view is that it presents the universe, and innumerable other possible universes, as already having run their courses, albeit in conditional form. From the sum total of all these conditions, God selects (he actualizes) some of them in order to actualize one universe. But this is a false picture. The universe cannot, given the strong view of freedom endorsed by the Molinists, have a shadow form; a form of a purely conditional kind which is the mirror-image of how the universe will be when it is actual. For how it will be when it is actual is, at least in part, up to the free actions of the agents who are actualized, once God has decided to actualize that universe.

We should not be seduced by the picture. God could not 'steer' the course of events in this fashion, given that all the while the individuals in the actualized universe have indeterministic freedom. For the circumstances never ensure one determinate freely-chosen outcome; they provide only the conditions for the free choice of one of several outcomes. Hence God cannot 'weakly actualize'[20] certain outcomes; he cannot, that is, use his knowledge of what a free creature would do under certain circumstances to achieve a desired end.

William Lane Craig, in a particularly clear exposition of the position, distinguishes three logical 'moments' in the actualizing of the world. The second of these moments corresponds to God's middle knowledge. Craig claims that

> in the second moment, which corresponds to God's middle knowledge, those aspects of the actual world exist which are states of affairs concerning what free creatures would do in any set of circumstances. For example in this second moment the state of affairs 'if Jones were placed in circumstances c, then he would freely do action X' is actual. Of course,

neither Jones nor the circumstances yet exist, except as ideas in God's mind. But it is nevertheless the case that if Jones were to be actualized by God and placed in c, then Jones would freely do x. Thus the states of affairs which are expressed by true counterfactuals concerning free decisions by humans are in fact already actual at this second moment. So even though at this moment the actual world in all its fullness does not yet exist, nonetheless certain aspects of it already exist, namely logically necessary states of affairs and states of affairs corresponding to true counterfactuals concerning creaturely freedom.[21]

Thus Craig asserts that prior to God's decision to create a world, all the features of the world he is to create, including all the outcomes of the free decisions of his creatures, are present to his mind. All that God has to do in creating the world is to make such definite actualities (which exist in his mind) exist in fact. But it is just this seductive picture of God's relation to possibility that must be resisted, because, given human indeterministic freedom, it cannot be true. As William Hasker puts it in criticizing the view, 'insofar as an agent is genuinely free, there *are* no true counterfactuals stating what the agent would definitely do under various possible circumstances.'[22]

The source of this confusion may lie in a failure to distinguish between abstract possibilities and concrete actualities. There are, in the mind of God, sets of abstract possibilities, for example, the idea of a certain possible person. In creating an actual person, however, God creates all his or her physical and psychological powers, and much else besides. Creation is not like opening the door of a cage to free a lion; it is the bringing of the lion into being.[23]

We may also be misled by an analogy to draw the opposite conclusion. We frequently say that we know our friends so well that we definitely know what they would choose in a given set of circumstances. If we know, surely God can know? But this is to forget, not only that God's knowledge is infallible, but also that if our friends are genuinely free, then in any given circumstances, they are free to choose the opposite course of action from the one that we believe, on the basis of past experience, they will in fact choose.

There are then possibilities – about the outcome of indeterministic free choices – which God does not know completely. Accordingly, he cannot instantiate complete possibilities respecting anyone's free choice. And so, because his middle knowledge of such free choices is necessarily incomplete, he cannot exercise a 'no-risk' providential control over his creation via his middle knowledge.

We began this discussion by referring to God's omniscience. But God's omniscience is limited by what is knowable. If Jones is indeterministically free, then it is not knowable, either to God or to us or to any other observer, what Jones will do when, in a given set of circumstances, he is confronted with a choice.

Does this somehow involve a limit upon God's omniscience? Are we saying that there are truths that God cannot know? Different answers have been given to this question. Swinburne, as we have seen, believes that God freely denies himself the knowledge of what he could know. Others argue that until Jones, as a free agent, has actually made his free decision, there is nothing *to know*. And because there is nothing to know, there is nothing for God to know. So, far from middle knowledge being a way of reconciling divine omniscience (and foreordination) and human freedom, we must conclude that human freedom limits the scope of divine omniscience.

Such a state of affairs would not preclude God from making an informed guess, an expert guess, about what Jones is likely to do. Perhaps, in circumstances C, it is very probable that Jones will do A. But the knowledge of such probabilities falls well short of that infallibility which is classically predicated of God, and which the proponents of middle knowledge certainly wish to portray him as possessing.[24]

An antinomy?

The appeal to middle knowledge is ambitious. It attempts to preserve both indeterministic freedom, and a 'no-risk' view of providence extending to all particular actions, by demonstrating such compatibility via God's middle knowledge. The approach we shall now consider could be said to attempt to achieve the same result, but by altogether different and more modest means.

It is acknowledged on all hands that the relation between divine action and human actions is *incomprehensible* – not that it is impossible to understand anything whatsoever about that relation, but that we can never hope fully to understand or to explain how it is possible to preserve both the sovereignty and independence of God, and human responsibility and accountability. The proponents of middle knowledge would no doubt recognize this, as do the proponents of other views to be considered later.

It is possible to argue, however, that the issue of divine sovereignty and human accountability is such a difficult one that it is unwise to expend the effort necessary to gain even a modest understanding of it. Rather, we should simply accept that Scripture teaches both, and leave it at that.

In *Evangelism and the Sovereignty of God*, J. I. Packer takes what is in effect this position by calling divine sovereignty and human responsibility an *antinomy*:

> The whole point of an antinomy – in theology, at any rate – is that it is not a real contradiction, though it looks like one. It is an *apparent* incompatibility between two apparent truths. An antinomy exists when a pair of principles stand side by side, seemingly irreconcilable, yet both undeniable. There are cogent reasons for believing each of them; each rests on clear and solid evidence; but it is a mystery to you how they can be squared with each other. You see that each must be true on its own, but you do not see how they can both be true together.[25]

> Man is a responsible moral agent, though he is *also* divinely controlled; man is divinely controlled, though he is *also* a responsible moral agent. God's sovereignty is a reality, and man's responsibility is a reality too.[26]

The antinomy which we face now is only one of a number that the Bible contains. We may be sure that they all find their reconciliation in the mind and counsel of God, and we may hope that in heaven we shall understand them ourselves. But meanwhile, our wisdom is to maintain with equal emphasis both the apparently conflicting truths in each case, to hold them together in the relation in which the Bible itself sets them, and to recognize that here is a mystery which we cannot expect to solve in this world.[27]

There are a number of things worth noting about these positions. In the first place, in terms of the basic categorization that we are using in this chapter, Packer is taking a 'no-risk' view of providence. This is clear from his statement that man is divinely controlled, and from the fact that he recognizes that there is a problem of an acute kind here. There would be no problem were he prepared to dilute the claim about divine control. It is only because of this control (and because of human responsibility) that there is a problem in the first place. What Packer is saying, in effect, is that given that there is a 'no-risk' view of divine providence, it is impossible to see how this can be reconciled with the view that human beings are responsible for their actions.

According to Packer, the difficulty about reconciling divine sovereignty and human responsibility is due to our ignorance. It is important to see that he is not arguing that the difficulty arises because of some basic contradictoriness about the nature of things. He is not arguing that the claims that God is sovereign and that men and women are responsible are logically contradictory – like the claims that Smith is to the left of Robinson and Robinson to the left of Smith. On the contrary, he is emphasizing that the sovereignty of God and the responsibility of men and women must be consistent, since both are true. The point is, though, that from our present vantage point we cannot see how they can be consistent.

There are different kinds of ignorance. I may know your name but not your telephone number. This ignorance of mine is, however, fairly easily remedied, for I can look up your number in the directory. Even if your number is ex-directory I can obtain it from you. We might call this contingent ignorance.

Such contingent ignorance can be contrasted with necessary ignorance. We do not know what a shrimp's view of a barnacle is, or what it is like to be a bat. This is because we are not shrimps or bats, and are *necessarily* not shrimps or bats. In a similar way, it is impossible for us to know what it is like to be God, and to have his timeless vision of his creation. There are hosts of such matters of which we are necessarily ignorant.

Yet Packer is not arguing that among the things of which we are necessarily ignorant is the recognition of the consistency of God's sovereign control of human beings and their personal responsibility. For he expresses the hope that, in heaven, Christians will understand every antinomy presented to them in the Bible, including the antinomy of divine sovereignty and human responsibility. Yet Packer seems to be saying that our ignorance, though not absolutely necessary, is necessary in this life. This is either because there are data relevant to the reconciliation of the antinomy which are withheld from us, or because our faculties of understanding are constricted in some way in this life (or for both of these reasons).

What are we to make of Packer's proposal that, in effect, Christians should confess both divine 'no-risk' providence and human responsibility, admit their ignorance, and leave the matter there?

The proposal does have several strengths. It sacrifices nothing in terms of the positions that a Christian might wish to hold on this issue. There are no theoretical constraints or considerations ruling out any particular position. In the construction of Christian doctrine there is always the danger of rationalism, of imposing some *a priori* principle upon the data from which the doctrine is to be constructed or restricting a doctrine to what we can understand about it. Clearly enough, Packer's proposal avoids such dangers. By the same token – and this is the second of its strengths – Packer can take into account the full range of the scriptural data in an uninhibited fashion, reserving any difficulties that the consideration of such data raises until, in heaven, we possess the necessary faculties, or additional data, or both.

These are considerable gains. Yet there are a number of disadvantages to be set against them. As we have seen, Packer affirms that certain biblical doctrines constitute antinomies. But by what means is it established that there is an antinomy? Packer says that 'it is forced upon us by the facts themselves'.[28] But how do we establish the difference between facts which are very hard to reconcile, and facts which are antinomic in character? Clearly it is not sufficient to say that in the one case the facts do not force an antinomic conclusion, whereas in the other case they do. Packer has reasoned his way to the conclusion that certain data constitute an antinomy. But the process of his reasoning is unclear.

Whatever the details of that reasoning, in order to be justified it will have to have included a general statement to the effect that all reasonable steps have been taken to reconcile the two claims about divine sovereignty and human responsibility, and have failed. The number of failures of reconciliation must be sufficiently large to generate the conclusion, on inductive grounds, that it is reasonable to believe that the two claims are antinomic in character. But has such an enquiry ever been undertaken?

The second difficulty is perhaps the more serious. Packer distinguishes between an antinomy and a self-contradiction or logical incoherence. An antinomy is an apparent inconsistency, not a real one. But it is an apparent inconsistency which, in this life, we shall be for ever unable to clear up. There is no way of effecting a reconciliation, and we know that there is no such way. But then, in these circumstances, what is the difference between an apparent inconsistency and a real one? How do we know that what is called an antinomy might not turn out to be a real inconsistency?

Packer would presumably reply to the question by an appeal to Scripture. He might argue that since both divine sovereignty and human responsibility are taught in Scripture, and are divinely revealed truths, they must be consistent, since truth is one. Nothing that is divinely revealed can be inconsistent with anything else that is divinely revealed, however much it may seem to us to be inconsistent.

The problem with such a reply is that it is too permissive. During the history of Christianity there is scarcely a limit to the nonsense that has been believed because it is allegedly biblical in character. No doubt the doctrines of divine providence and human responsibility are centrally biblical in a way that other themes are not. Nevertheless, in the light of what has happened in history, it may be thought that some attempt ought to be made to show their consistency.

In fact, even in Packer's brief treatment of the issue, and despite what he says about simply accepting the antinomy, there are traces of an attempt to provide some of this reasoning. Thus it is interesting, and surely significant, that Packer does not speak in terms of human *freedom* but of human *responsibility*. Yet there is nothing in his appeal to the idea of an antinomy that would prevent him arguing that divine sovereignty and human indeterministic freedom constitute an antinomy. He contents himself with referring to responsibility only, and says nothing about the conditions for human responsibility. So, although appealing to an antinomy could be a licence for accepting nonsense (or, to be more polite, for accepting statements of a strongly counter-intuitive nature), Packer restricts his use of it.

It ought to be emphasized that these critical comments are not offered as decisive against Packer's approach. Its attractions remain, and readers must make up their own minds as to which approach to take. Nevertheless, because of the theoretical unsatisfactoriness of appealing to an antinomy, an attempt will be made to take the discussion a stage further.

Compatibilism

We have looked at several ways in which a 'no-risk' view of providence might be established (notably by appealing either to middle knowledge or by invoking the idea of an antinomy), and have found difficulties with each. In the case of middle knowledge, the difficulty is with the indeterministic view of freedom its proponents adopt. In the case of the idea of an antinomy, the difficulty lies with its theoretically permissive stance.

In the history of debate about human freedom and responsibility, two contrasting views of freedom have been identified: indeterministic freedom (sometimes referred to as the liberty of indifference), and deterministic freedom (sometimes referred to as the liberty of spontaneity). As we have noted, the attractiveness of the middle-knowledge approach lies in its assumption that human freedom requires the liberty of indifference. By contrast, the view taken in what follows favours deterministic freedom. According to this view, people perform free acts when they do what they want to do, not when they have the power of self-causation, or some other version of indeterminism. That is, they are not constrained or compelled in their actions, but what they do flows unimpededly from their wants, desires, preferences, goals and the like.

The great advantage of such a view of human freedom is that, being compatible with determinism, it is also compatible with a full view of divine omniscience and omnipotence, and thus with a 'no-risk' theory of providence. Possible disadvantages lie in the areas of human responsibility and the problem of evil. We shall attempt to handle these difficulties in later chapters. It is perhaps sufficient at this stage to indicate the assumption upon which the subsequent discussion rests.

Needless to say, the policy of taking up one position, sticking to it, and following through its consequences, is not intended to constrain the reader. Authors naturally hope that whoever reads their books will end up holding views corresponding to those set out in them. But whether or not my readers conclude by holding a 'risk-free' view of divine providence, and the compatibilist view of human freedom and determinism which I believe most naturally coheres with it, the important thing is that readers make up their own minds in the light of the evidence presented to them.

Each of the views just discussed (middle knowledge, the antinomic view, and compatibilism), is consistent with the 'no-risk' view of divine providence. Each position has its own strengths and weaknesses which have repercussions in other areas of Christian theology. In following this study as it traces some of the repercussions of compatibilism, readers will no doubt wish to keep the other views in mind as alternatives. It is hoped that the discussion of this chapter will make it easier for them, if they find themselves disagreeing with the main thread of argument, to make the necessary adjustments to it, and thus, by the end, to have developed a view of divine providence of their own which they believe to be Christian, coherent, and defensible.[29]

3

THE THEOLOGICAL
FRAMEWORK

In the first chapter, we introduced three contexts in which questions about divine providence, God's activity now, can arise. These are the contexts of personal guidance, of the life and history of the Christian church, and of the nature of God's relation to the world. It is obvious that the last of these is the most general and the most basic of the three, and accordingly we shall consider it first. The other two contexts presuppose an account of the relation of God to the world. The exact character of that relationship will clearly constrain the character of the other two contexts.

For example, if it were established that God's relation to the universe was such that miracles were either impossible or unnecessary, then this would have a significant effect on how God's providential care of the Christian church is to be understood. Again, if it could be established that God's relationship to his universe were one of profound unconcern on his part, then petitionary prayer could play no part in personal guidance.

It is sometimes supposed that the question of God's relation to the universe is a *scientific* one that can be addressed by cosmology. If scientists were to solve the riddle of whether the physical origins of the universe lay in a Big Bang, or whether the universe exists in a steady state, then it is thought that we should come nearer to explaining the relationship between God and the physical universe.

It is fundamentally important, not only for the topic of this chapter, but for the whole concept of divine providence, to be clear why this is not so. If God's relation to the physical universe is capable of being understood scientifically, then God would be part of the physical universe. Investigating God and the universe would be like investigating the relationship of one planet to another, or of one galaxy to another, or the relationship of anything physical to anything else that is physical. But, according to Scripture, God is not a part of the physical universe, an individual who can be understood as an immense source of physical power. Rather, God is the *creator* of the entire physical universe. He is not a part of it, but the author of it. In the language of theology, God *transcends* the universe.

Some objects occupy a great deal of space and a great deal of time; others less so. But it makes no sense to ask where in space and time the universe is. For this would be to suppose that the universe were a part of some yet larger physical dimension. The idea that the universe began to exist at some moment in time suggests that there were events occurring before the creation of the universe. But if such events did occur, they would be a part of the universe, not separate from it.

This also applies to the creation. The 'beginning' mentioned in Genesis 1:1, if it refers to the creation of the entire physical universe, cannot refer to an event, like the beginning of a football match or the onset of a disease. Such beginnings *presuppose* space and time. It is plausible to suppose, however, that in the creation of the universe, space and time were themselves created, since they relate together what is created. As Augustine put it:

> The way, God, in which you made heaven and earth was not that you made them either in heaven or on earth. Nor was it in air or in water, for these belong

to heaven and earth. Nor did you make the universe
within the framework of the universe. There was
nowhere for it to be made before it was brought into
existence.[1]

Thus, when we say that God existed before the universe,
the 'before' is not temporal but hierarchical in meaning. It
means something like this: the universe might not have
existed, and depends for its existence upon God, and God
does not depend for his existence on anything.

So the question of God's relation to the universe is not a
scientific question. Then what sort of a question is it? It is a
metaphysical or ontological question. For in considering this
issue we are asking fundamental questions about the nature
of being or reality, even more fundamental than those asked,
say, by the physicist or chemist. The task of the physicist or
chemist is to analyse the physical character of the universe, its
basic physical properties and history. Ontological questions
concern the relationship of one *sort* of being to another or
others. Thus one of the mental disciplines that has to be
cultivated in considering such questions is to avoid physical
ways of thinking, or at least to recognize them for what they
are – analogies and models which only imperfectly, and some
times misleadingly, represent the true account.

But if the idea of creation is not scientific, neither is it
mythical. The Christian wishes to maintain that it is *true* that
the universe was (or is) created by God. But if it is true, then it
cannot be a myth. For myths, in at least one central
understanding of that word, are not true or false. They are
guiding ideas which are to be retained or rejected in
accordance with whether or not they are useful or
illuminating in some way. The question of whether or not the
universe is created is either true or false. It is, therefore,
something that can in principle be known. If it is true, then
God knows it, and others may.

Pantheism and deism

There are a relatively few possible ways in which God's
relation to the universe can be understood. One of these,

pantheism, is full of interest, and has from time to time been influential. It is not a view, though, that could command acceptance from the Christian. For pantheism is the view that the universe *is* God. Such a view is not acceptable to the Christian because it denies the distinction between God and the universe, and disallows the very idea of creation. For one fundamental feature of the creation is that the creatures are distinct from their creator, and depend upon him for their existence.

This distinctness can be expressed in the following way. An object is ontologically distinct from God if there is at least one property which God has, but which the object lacks, or vice versa. That is true of all objects which we regard as having been created. For example, God is infinitely good, but even the holiest saint is not that good. The holiest saint occupies a particular region of space, but God does not occupy regions of space, nor could he. And what is true of properties is true of actions. If pantheism were true, and the universe just *is* God, then (presumably) when an individual in the universe performed an action, it would follow that God performed that action, or perhaps that the action was (in some rather obscure sense) performed *in* God. But when Neville Chamberlain attempted to appease Hitler, God did not appease Hitler. Nor, when Hitler refused to be appeased by Chamberlain, did God refuse to be appeased by Chamberlain. Nor did these exchanges take place in God. It is an implication of the Christian view of creation that Chamberlain and Hitler were two distinct individuals, each created and upheld by God, and under the providential control of God. For that very reason they are not to be regarded as being identical with God, but distinct from him.

This distinctness emerges most vividly, perhaps, in the case of responsibility for good and evil – particularly evil. Although Hitler was created and sustained by God, and his unholy career was under the superintendence of God, nevertheless, when Hitler sinned, God did not sin, and could not sin. But if pantheism is true, whatever is attributable to the universe is attributable to God. So if in the universe Hitler sins, then in that respect at least God sins, or is at the very least imperfect.

Not only does pantheism deny the distinctness of God and his creation; it also obviously excludes the idea of any inter-action between them, for it is impossible for one thing to interact with itself.

For these reasons, but chiefly because it flouts the basic Christian idea of the ontological distinctness of God from his creation, pantheism is not a serious option.

Nor are matters any better in the case of panentheism, the theory that the universe, while not identical with God, is an extension or emanation of him. This view, associated most prominently with 'process' theology, preserves the logical distinctness of God and his creation, and so is to be distinguished from pantheism. For the panentheist, God is not identical with the universe. Nevertheless, the universe does not depend for its existence on the free choice of God, but is an inevitable emanation of his goodness. This rules out any interaction between the creator and his creatures.

But another possible relation, deism, has proved immensely popular and influential. The label 'deism' is used deliberately, but care is needed in understanding it. For it is not easy to extract the 'deistic' view of God's relation to the world from the writings of the deists, that group of freethinking religious philosophers which flourished in England in the eighteenth century. This is because they tended to adopt a negative theological method. They argued against special revelation and miracle while at the same time supporting, and being supported by, the rise of Newtonian science. It is by extrapolation from their expressed views that the deistic idea of God's relation to the universe is to be understood.

Deism states that God created the universe in accordance with certain physical laws, and that, by the inherent power with which it is endowed at the creation, it thereafter behaves in a regular, law-like way. God could have created a universe in accordance with other laws, but the laws which he actually chose to use underline his wisdom. As the philosopher Leibniz put it:

> God created substances and gives them the force they
> need, and after that he leaves them to themselves and
> does nothing but conserve them in their actions.[2]

73

The questions whether, according to deism, these physical laws extend to all aspects of the creation (human beings included), and whether the universe, once created, will persist indefinitely, are issues which can be left to one side. What is of importance and of interest is the idea of the universe being endowed with certain powers which then inherently persist. We shall critically examine this claim later in the chapter.

It will be noted that, whatever its defects may prove to be from the Christian point of view, deism is a considerable improvement upon pantheism. It emphatically asserts the distinctness of God from his creation. This comes out clearly in the deist's contention that any creature is endowed with certain powers or properties in terms of which it acts and interacts with other creatures in a law-like way. The question is not whether the deist insists on the distinctness between God and the creation, but whether he overstates it.

Let us try to understand more exactly what the deist claims by considering some illustrations. If a player strikes a snooker ball with a cue, then the force imparted to the ball ensures that it moves across the table in a certain direction, at a certain speed (unless something else, such as another snooker ball, intervenes). All that is necessary for the ball to move is that it is struck, and that certain physical laws obtain and continue to obtain. Due to friction and resistance of various other kinds, the ball slows down and eventually stops. The snooker player, having struck the ball, need play no further part in ensuring that it follows a certain path. Indeed, to play any further part would ensure that it did not follow that path. The snooker player, having set the ball in motion, is thereafter a spectator.

If we suppose (rather implausibly, perhaps) that the snooker player had also designed and manufactured the ball, the cue and the table, and (even less plausibly) had in some way established the laws of force and momentum which the struck and moving ball observes, then this total picture begins to resemble the deistic view of God's relation to the universe. God is the *originator of and imparter of movement* to the universe and all that it contains. Having imparted the movement, there is no need for him to intervene to adapt or to modify the original plan – no need to intervene, that is, because not only does God have the requisite power to do all this, but he is also sufficiently wise and good to arrange things in such a way that no intervention will henceforth be necessary (according to the deist). It is not so much that God *could* not intervene once the original created order had been set going, but rather, because he has wisely and beneficently set it going, there is *no need* for him to intervene to augment or to correct what he has done. Behind deism there thus stands both a particular view of God's relation to the physical universe and a particular view of his character.

We might express this in more formal terms as follows. If a created object O has powers pl-pn at tl, then unless God intervenes (which he has no good reason to do) O will, in virtue of God's conservation of it, have powers pl-pn at all subsequent periods of its existence.

This schema fits best where O is the entire physical creation. For if O is an object within the creation, then any schema has to allow for the fact that O may cease to exist, and that before O ceases to exist, it may physically decay and become weaker and less potent, or grow and become stronger. It is no part of deism to argue that everything that is created never ceases to exist. The position does argue, however, that things which cease to exist and start to exist do so in virtue of more powers in the universe, and that these basic powers are a primitive and enduring endowment of the physical universe. Therefore, if, as a result of the planting of a seed in the ground, a tree grows, then though the tree is a new thing, the physical powers in virtue of which the seed germinates and grows are a part of the original endowment of the universe.

What are the consequences of such a view for the idea of divine providence? If one considers different possible doctrines of divine providence along a spectrum, then there are two extreme positions. One is that of a god who, having created the universe, is utterly careless or unconcerned as to its fate. For all he knows or cares, the universe might degenerate into utter chaos. For obvious reasons such a view could not seriously be considered as an option by the Christian. The other extreme is of a god who, in creating the universe, creates it in such a way that he does not *need* to exercise a superintending care of it. This is the deistic view. But such a view creates two areas of difficulty for the Christian.

According to the Christian faith, one of the ways in which God has acted upon his creation is through miracles, direct actions upon physical nature which are without precedent. Thus, on occasion, God causes the waves of the Red Sea to part, the jaws of the lions to remain shut, the ravens to provide meat; crucially, he raises Christ from the dead. We shall have more to say later about the place of miracles in providence, but it is important to note that, on the deistic view, God has no need to act in such a way.

A deist would agree that, considered in the abstract, God doubtless has the power to work miraculously. For if he has the power to create the universe, then it is plausible to assume that he has the power to alter what he has made. According to the deist, though, God has no *need* to work miraculously, because such an act would betoken a lack of foresight or wisdom on his part, something which is unthinkable to the deist. Miracles, on this view, are afterthoughts – tinkerings with and tunings of an engine that, given the power and competence of the engineer, should never need to arise and will never arise. (Those thinkers such as Leibniz, aspects of whose thought are deistic, allow a place for miracles provided that they are understood as part of God's pre-established harmony between the realms of nature and of grace.)

From the standpoint of the Christian faith, however, this is a piece of utter dogmatism. It is not appropriate to argue, *a priori*, what God will and will not do with and in the physical creation, but – as with any contingent matter of fact – it is necessary to investigate what God has done. The Christian church, bearing testimony to divine revelation, affirms that God has in fact acted miraculously. And since he has acted miraculously he must have had a good reason to do so.

It may seem that deism is a position of historical interest only. But, in his Bampton Lectures,[3] Maurice Wiles defends a view that is remarkably similar to that of the deists. The view might be labelled 'continuous deism'. What makes it deistic is

76

that God's relation to the universe is limited to bringing it into existence. Wiles argues that

> For the theist, who is necessarily committed to a unitary view of the world, the whole process of the bringing into being of the world, which is still going on, needs to be seen as one action of God.[4]

Like the deists, Wiles does not claim that miracles are inconceivable. He argues that it is necessary to 'abandon the concept of miracle as a distinct form of direct divine causation' on religious grounds: if miracles are regarded as occasional interventions by God, they raise the question why God does not intervene more frequently and more crucially in human affairs. We shall take up this question in the later chapter on providence and evil. But Wiles also endorses the position of Brian Hebblethwaite that it is

> not unreasonable to suppose that even the Incarnation is achieved without breaking the structures of the natural world.[5]

In so far as this supposition is made on metaphysical grounds, it would appear to rest upon a confusion. For there is a perfectly good sense in which the universe is unitary (one action of God); namely, in the sense that it proceeds from the one will or decree of God. From God's point of view, each aspect of that one act is equally willed and equally 'natural'. All is part of one structure. But it may still be that, when measured by human experience, some of these aspects are miraculous, unparalleled or unprecedented activities. But such events, unparalleled from a human point of view, are not 'interventions' in the sense that they are God's second thoughts, bespeaking a need to violate or to repair the effects of his first thoughts. As we shall shortly see, it is a mistake to restrict the elements of God's upholding of the universe to his preparedness, or otherwise to his 'intervening' by performing miracles.

A second area of difficulty concerns the place of prayer in divine providence. According to the Christian faith, God answers petitionary prayer. That is, certain things happen in the universe only because people ask God that they happen, and God is pleased to do what they ask. Had they not asked, the event in question would not have occurred; or at least, had they not asked, there is no reason to think that the event would have occurred.

A deist, however, (at least, if he is consistent) will find no place for such petitionary prayer. The reason for this is as before: to suppose that God might answer petitionary prayer is to suppose that he might *need* to do so. Such a supposition is (according to the deist) inconsistent with the power and wisdom of God. If God is supremely wise and powerful, how could he need to be prompted by a prayer into doing something that there is already good reason to do? For either there is good reason to perform that event prayed for (in which case praying is otiose, for God will perform the action anyway); or there is no good reason to perform the event prayed for (in which case praying for the event to happen is pointless, for all such prayers will be requests for God to be less than wholly wise, which he cannot be).

Once again, the root of the deistic attitude lies in an *a priori* view of what God can and cannot do, or of what it is reasonable for God to do or not to do. The relation of prayer to divine providence raises acute problems, to which we give attention later on. But no approach to such problems can (as the deist 'solution' proposes) subvert the warrant the Christian has from Scripture to pray for certain things in order to obtain them.

Nor does it seem a valid objection to the idea of a miraculous event that such an event raises problems of interpretation for the human observer of it, or for one who seeks to offer comment upon it. The first question must be, what are miracles? And then, can miracles occur? Then it is necessary to enquire whether they have in fact occurred. Only if and when the last question has been answered in the affirmative is it appropriate to enter into the difficulties that these data may present for interpretation. The interpretation must follow the events in question. It cannot determine whether those events did or did not take place.

Perhaps enough has been said about deism both to provide

a flavour of its essence and to indicate something of its extreme unsatisfactoriness for the Christian.

The attractions of deism

Despite such weaknesses, deistic ways of thinking exercise a considerable hold over the minds of Christians who would, nevertheless, not subscribe to deism's extreme rationalism. The continuing power of deism lies in the fact that it presents God's relation to the universe in a way which can readily be thought of in human terms: the artist and the artefact, the engineer and the machine, and so on. This picture can be sketched in the following terms:

> God existed, and then, 'in the beginning', he created the physical universe;

or

> God existed before the physical universe which he created.

Given that all our experience is of actions taking place in time, it is natural that we should think of God creating the universe in time. Once we do that, unless we guard our thinking very carefully, we are only a step away from a deistic conception of God's relation to the universe; so close to deism, in fact, that it becomes necessary to issue anti-deistic disclaimers: 'God has not abandoned the universe which he has made', 'God still controls the universe', and so on.

In the second statement above, the 'before' is a temporal 'before'; the 'and then' of the first statement also expresses a temporal relation. This is utterly congenial to the deist. But deism is avoided, indeed made impossible, if the 'before' in 'God is before the universe' is regarded as an ontological or hierarchical 'before'. When we state that, in constitutional importance, the Queen is before the Prime Minister, it is clear that the 'before' is not temporal, but hierarchical. God is before the universe, not in the sense that he existed at a time before the universe was created, but in the sense that he is timelessly eternal, and independent of the universe. The universe, by contrast, is in time, and dependent upon God. Nothing was before (in time) the beginning of the universe, but God exists eternally, and the universe exists by his eternal will.

It is true that many who are not deists are 'temporalists', holding the view that God is in time and that he created the universe at some time. They maintain that 'the beginning' is not ontological but temporal in character.[6] Nevertheless, such thinkers find it more difficult than 'eternalists' to avoid deism, and, because deism is at odds with biblical Christianity at vital points, this is an important negative consequence of 'temporalism'.

One thing that is sometimes said to be in favour of deism is that it preserves the transcendence of God over his creation, even though it can find no place for the biblical insistence upon God's immanence. But, in view of what we have been considering, this is hardly accurate. Certainly the deist has a clear sense of the distinctness of God from his creation. Nevertheless, a question must be raised as to whether this distinctness is a true transcendence. According to Christian theism, God transcends the universe not merely by being separate from it but by being its eternal, independent, uncreated ground.

In the foregoing discussion, certain features of Christian theism have already been foreshadowed. It is now time to look at theism more systematically. We argue for it as the concept which best captures the biblical position and provides the most adequate understanding of the most basic context of interest in which questions about divine providence arise.

Theism

It is a fundamental consequence of the biblical doctrine of creation that God is not to be identified with his creation. As we noted earlier, we might express this distinctness, in formal terms, as follows:

> If A and B exist, and are distinct from each other,
> then it is necessarily the case that there is some

80

proposition that is true of A and that is not true of B.

Thus, that God is distinct from me is proved by the fact that I am sitting at my wordprocessor but God is not. While this is true, however, it is not very illuminating regarding God's distinctness from his creation. For any two things (say me and my wordprocessor) are also distinct in precisely the same sense. There are truths about my wordprocessor that are not truths about me, and vice versa.

How then can we capture the distinctness between God and his creation? Perhaps as follows: God is in a special relation of distinctness to every other individual thing, whether these things are regarded individually or collectively. This relation is such that God is related to everything else in this way; they are not related to God in this way, and nothing that is not God is related to anything else that is not God in this way. The relation in question is that of *being continuously dependent upon.*

Thus my wordprocessor depends for its existence upon God, but God does not depend for his existence upon the wordprocessor. Nor does my wordprocessor depend upon me, or upon any other created thing, for its continued existence. This applies to every other object in the universe, and indeed to the universe as a whole. The universe depends upon God for its existence, but God does not depend upon the universe for his existence. Indeed God does not depend upon anything for his existence; he is independent and self-sufficient.

But it might be objected that my wordprocessor does not depend upon God for its existence, but upon the designers, engineers and manufacturers who, together, are responsible for its creation. Its existence depends also upon the properties of plastic, metal and microchips. If it is dependent upon them for its existence, how can it be dependent upon God as well? To change the example: I am dependent upon my parents for my existence; how then can I be dependent upon God?

We are already familiar with the deists' answer to these questions. But we have rejected this answer for reasons that do not need to be repeated.

How then is my wordprocessor dependent upon God?

Clearly, it is dependent not only in being made of materials which were created by God, but also by being in some sense *upheld* by God. Not only is the wordprocessor upheld by God, but the materials out of which it is made, and those designers and engineers who produced it, are or were similarly upheld by God.

This is the clear scriptural teaching. Paul, speaking at Athens, claims that 'we live and move and have our being' in God (Acts 17:28). Writing to the Colossian Christians, he emphasizes the 'cosmic Christ'; Jesus Christ is the one in whom 'all things hold together' (Col. 1:17). In John's terminology he is the Word: 'without him nothing was made that has been made' (Jn. 1:3). He is the one through whom God made the universe (Heb. 1:2).

'In some sense upheld by God.' The exact sense in which objects which are distinct from God are yet upheld by him is difficult to get clear. As with many theological doctrines, it is easier to say what this does not mean than what it does mean, and perhaps we shall have to be content with that. Once again, it is important to remember that we are not attempting to develop theories like scientific explanations, but to mark off the biblical data in as coherent and consistent a fashion as possible. The various attempts that have been made to clarify the nature of this 'upholding' will be considered in detail in a later chapter, when we turn our attention to the difficult question of the relation between God's action and the actions of his creatures (particularly people) for which they are responsible.

It is important to preserve what might be termed the 'vertical' dimension of God's relation to his creation, and indeed to stress this against the deistic view of God as the prime mover. Not only do the actions of my fingers cause words and phrases to appear on the screen of the wordprocessor, but also God upholds that whole process. He keeps my fingers and the wordprocessor in being, even while the words are produced by my fingers. Without this conserving power, what exists now would cease to exist.

If this vertical dimension is kept in mind, then the concept of a miracle is not a problem. For a miracle is then simply the way in which God has chosen to uphold the universe at that moment. Whether he chooses to uphold the universe by giving some aspect of it a character which is (by human experience) unprecedented is clearly a matter for his wisdom and goodness. God does not have to 'overcome' or 'violate' the laws of nature. But if our thinking is exclusively 'horizontal', and if we think of laws of nature as in some sense inviolable regulations laid down by the creator 'at the beginning', then the very idea of a miracle becomes problematic.

Yet, in stressing the vertical aspect of God's relation to the creation, we must not stress it to the point that we compromise the 'horizontal' causal relations (exemplified by my production of words on the wordprocessor screen) How could this vertical aspect compromise horizontal causal relations? By arguing that the divine sustaining of the universe through time is the only true *causal* relation in the entire universe, and hence that the actions and events which we normally think of as causes and effects are something else.

The intuitive idea of a cause is that which brings about another event or events, that is, the effect(s). Thus the motion of one snooker ball coming into contact with another, stationary, snooker ball, imparts force to the second ball and causes it to move. Similarly, my depressing the wordprocessor keys causes, in a more complicated way, changes on the screen before me. Or so we think.

Besides a temptation to overstress the vertical dimension of God's relation to the universe, there have been two reasons why some theists have been tempted to deny or qualify this. The first has to do with what is regarded as a special case of causation – the causal effect of the mind upon the body. Suppose that I want to quench my thirst and reach for the glass. Under normal circumstances, the desire is regarded as the cause of the movement of my arm; it is what the movement of my arm is *due to*.

This, however, has perplexed philosophers. How can an event which is mental, and therefore non-physical, be the cause of something which is physical and therefore non-mental? Where does the physical energy required to move my arm come from? Where does the causal event take place? In some part of my body? Which part? In no part of my body? Where, then?

> Now it appears to me quite certain that the will of minds is incapable of moving the smallest body in the world; for it is clear that there is no necessary connection between our will to move our arms, for example, and the movement of our arms. It is true that they are moved when we will it, and that thus we are the natural cause of the movement of our arms. But *natural* causes are not true causes; they are only *occasionally* causes that act only through the forces and efficacy of the will of God, as I have just explained.[7]

Perplexities about the relation between the mind and the body led certain theistic thinkers, such as Malebranche (1638–1715), to cut the Gordian knot and to argue that mental acts such as desires do not cause anything. What happens is that God so arranges his creation that certain events are conjoined with other events. My desire for a drink is conjoined with the movement of my arm; it does not cause my arm to move; rather it is the *occasion* of my arm moving.

But Malebranche did not restrict occasionalism to relations between the mind and the body:

> Because the ball does not have the power to move itself, they should not judge that a ball in motion is the true and principal cause of the movement of the ball it finds in its path. They can judge only that the collision of the two balls is the occasion for the Author of all motion in matter to carry out the decree of his will, which is the universal cause of all things.[8]

Occasionalism has been regarded as a classic case of a cure being worse than a disease. It is not hard to see why. For if the relation of the mind to the body is mysterious, then that of the causal relation of God to his creation is equally, if not more, so.

A second reason for emphasizing the vertical dimension – the divine 'upholding' – has lain in the concern of some theologians to stress the *immediacy* of the creation's reliance upon its creator. The divine upholding which, we have been arguing, is an integral part of Christian theism, might be expressed as follows:

> Whatever exists at one time can only continue to exist at any subsequent time if at that time God wills its existence.

Thus, my wordprocessor, which exists at 4:00 pm (let us suppose), can exist at a moment immediately after 4:00 pm only if God decrees that it exists immediately subsequent to 4:00 pm. In upholding the object in this way, God of course upholds it together with all its causal and other powers.

From this position it is a short but significant step to claim that

> whatever exists at one moment exists only at that moment. Anything that exists subsequent to that moment must be created by God at that moment.

But this is a startlingly radical view. What it means is that whatever exists does so only for a moment. My familiar wordprocessor, which has been my companion for many months, is in fact no such thing. It is not one continuous wordprocessor, but a series of momentary wordprocessors, each the instantaneous creation of God. The wordprocessor at moment 1 is a different object from the wordprocessor at moment 2, and so on. More alarmingly, on this view, you and I are not, as we fondly imagine, individuals existing and developing over many years, but a set of momentary individuals, each succeeding the other like the successive frames of a motion picture.

This view was held and developed by the American theologian and philosopher Jonathan Edwards. He sought to emphasize that all of us are immediately dependent upon God for our existence, and hence for our continued existence.

> God's upholding created substance, or causing its existence in each successive moment, is altogether

equivalent to an *immediate production out of nothing*, at each moment, because its existence at this moment is not merely in part from God, but wholly from him; and not in any part, or degree, from its antecedent existence ... So that this effect differs not at all from the first creation, only *circumstantially*; as in first creation there had been no such act and effect of God's power before; whereas, his giving existence afterwards, *follows* preceding acts and effects of the same kind, in an established order.[9]

This is, of course, a preposterous view, for all sorts of reasons. But the chief reason, for our purposes, that it must be emphatically rejected is that there is no place in it for horizontal causation. Nothing that exists at a moment can cause any effect at a later moment, since what exists at that moment immediately ceases to exist and is replaced by another momentary individual, the product of immediate divine power. Whatever the motives that Edwards had, and whatever ingenuity he displayed in working out the implications of this view, the price it pays is unacceptable. Causation raises many philosophical perplexities, but the way to handle these is not to deny that nothing ever causes anything else. How then are we to hold the horizontal and the vertical dimensions of the divine upholding in true harmony?

There is a long and honourable tradition according to which there are both *primary* and *secondary* causes. The primary cause (or causes) is the divine upholding; the secondary causes are the causal powers of created things; the power of the seed to germinate, of a person to be angry or to walk down the street, and so on. This distinction is helpful provided that two points are borne in mind. The first is that these two sorts of cause are not in competition with each other. The primary cause is an enabling and sustaining cause, making possible secondary causes and setting bounds to them. The second point is that the primary cause is not an event in time, as the secondary causes are, but is an eternal cause which has the whole of the creation as its effect.

Such a view has been widespread in Christian theology both before and after the Reformation: in Aquinas, for example,

> If God provided for all things by himself and with-
> out intermediaries, all secondary causes would be
> put out of action.[10]

> God's Providence procures its effects through the
> operation of secondary causes.[11]

And in Calvin:

> The sun rises day by day; but it is God that enlight-
> ens the earth by his rays. The earth brings forth her
> fruits; but it is God that giveth bread, and it is God
> that giveth strength by the nourishment of that
> bread. In a word, as all inferior and secondary
> causes, viewed in themselves, veil like so many cur-
> tains the glorious God from our sight (which they
> too frequently do), the eye of faith must be cast up
> far higher, that it may behold the hand of God
> working by all these His instruments.[12]

The Westminster Confession of Faith states:

> God from all eternity did, by the most wise and holy
> counsel of his own will, freely and unchangeably
> ordain whatsoever comes to pass; yet so, as thereby
> neither is God the author of sin, nor is violence
> offered to the will of the creatures, nor is the liberty
> or contingency of second causes taken away, but
> rather established.[13]

On this view, then, God works through secondary causes.
They have no power independently of his working. Yet they
are truly causal. God, considered as the primary cause, is not
located within the created universe, but transcends it. We
shall look at this model of a hierarchy of causes more closely
in chapter 7.

To summarize what may seem to have been a rather tortu-
ous discussion: the theist (as opposed to the deist and the
pantheist) affirms *both* that God upholds the universe that he
has created, *and* that the universe contains within it agents

which have causal powers – different causal powers depending upon the kind of agent. To deny the divine upholding forces one to hold that the universe exists in virtue of powers with which it has been endowed in the past, and to commit oneself to a version of deism. To deny that the universe contains individuals with causal powers, besides being strongly counter-intuitive, has devastating implications for personal responsibility and accountability. For persons are responsible for what they *do*. If they do nothing, or are each (as Edwards claimed) nothing other than a set of momentary individuals, then the most they can be responsible for is only what they are capable of performing in that moment.

One objection that might be raised against the theistic view is that it confuses creation and providence. How can the view outlined above do justice to the divine 'resting', taught in the early chapters of Genesis and elsewhere? How can God be said to rest if he is continuously upholding the universe?

Certainly God cannot be said to rest if by 'rest' is meant inactivity and unconcern. But does the text mean this? What the resting means is that the creation has taken place. God does not continue to create. But he does uphold what he has created, not by creating it again and again but by sustaining it. Not only does he rest (Gn. 2:2), but he works (Jn. 5:17), and does not slumber or sleep (Ps. 121:4).[14]

Part of this activity, the divine upholding, involves the emergence of new things in the universe. As the universe unfolds in time, so individuals are born and die, there is evolution in nature; new objects (such as cars and planes) and new substances (such as alloys and plastics) are developed. But none of this is strictly *creative* activity. Rather it involves the forming of new individuals and substances out of what already exists, not creation from nothing. All such changes are under the superintendence of divine providence. So, although God has rested from the work of his creation, as the Sabbath-sign indicates, this rest does not imply that the universe is static and immobile. It does not betoken a deistic unconcern on God's part with what has been created and put in motion. What it does imply is that the amazing and unparalleled divine willing of the universe out of nothing is completed.

Another objection levelled against the theistic view is that the relation between the creator and creation is such a close and continuous one as to make the universe an *emanation* from God, something which by an inevitable process flows out of God. But there are a number of reasons why theism does not entail such a view. In the first place, emanation does not do justice to the place of God's reason and will in the creation. The material universe and all that it contains cannot be considered to be an extension of God. Rather, it is created by the free will and intention of God. God was not constrained in creating by any necessity external to himself, nor did creation have the causal inevitability of a natural process.

Even here it is necessary to preserve the correct balance. The universe was created by the free decision of God. Yet it would be wrong to suppose that that decision was a cold and calculating affair. As Aquinas put it, in creating, God wills 'to share his own goodness by making things as like to him as possible'.[15]

Conclusion

In this chapter we have been concerned with setting forth the broadest and most fundamental context in which the issue of divine providence may be raised: the divine creation and, particularly, the divine upholding of the universe.

It should be stressed that this upholding, being metaphysical or ontological in character, is physically undetectable. It is not a piece of religiously inspired natural science. It is not a scientific hypothesis which we may hope to confirm or discredit by conducting experiments or by making observations. Suppose that it is asserted that a particular bridge is held up by steel cables; it is possible to check this. But it is not possible in the same way to check the claim that the universe is upheld by the power of God, its creator.

What reason is there, then, for thinking that theism expresses the truth about God's relation to the universe? If it cannot be proved or disproved by scientific evidence, why ought we to believe it? This question can be answered at two levels.

In the first place, the reason for the Christian to believe it lies in the crucial part that this account plays in the *coherence* of the Christian faith. The doctrine of the divine transcendence of the universe, yet immanence within it, though not provable directly, is nevertheless a necessary condition of other matters which the Christian faith affirms. We have already touched on one of these in our attempt to elaborate the divine relation to the universe: namely, the Christian teaching about the creation of the universe *ex nihilo*. In addition, the Christian faith claims that God is the Lord of nature and the Lord of history. At crucial periods, at the various 'appointed' times, the Lord has acted in unprecedented fashion in the formation , preservation and deliverance of his ancient people Israel, and supremely in the incarnation. For when the time had fully come, God sent forth his Son. Without an understanding of God the creator as being at once transcendent over his creation and yet immanent within it, it is hard if not impossible to make sense of these other matters which are obviously critical for the intellectual integrity of the Christian faith.

Part of the reason for believing in God's immanence and transcendence – his providential rule of his universe – is therefore that it coheres in a straightforwardly logical and explanatory way with other crucial doctrines. But the question of evidence may still be pressed. Granted, someone might say, that one reason for believing in divine transcendence and immanence is the coherence of that doctrine with the Christian faith as a whole, is there nevertheless no more *direct* evidence of that upholding? Surely, if it is true, we might expect there to be such evidence – not *direct* evidence (we cannot expect to *see* the divine upholding, as if it were by steel cables). Nevertheless, may there not be indirect evidence? Would it not be strange if there were no indirect evidence at all?

Another, more familiar, way of phrasing this question is to ask: is there evidence in nature and in history of the existence of God? Those who answer in the affirmative commit themselves to some form of the 'argument from design' for God's existence. Perhaps, though, we are asking a more specific question than this. Is there evidence now that God is working now in the immanent way that theism affirms? There may or may not be general evidence from nature that there is a God, and that he has certain powers and character. But even if there is no such general evidence, it is nevertheless a legitimate question. Such evidence is sought, not as a proof of his existence, but as a reasonable consequence of it.

The testimony of Scripture is that there is evidence of God's activity in the natural occurrence of beneficial regularities in nature, for example, and particularly in the existence of the Christian church and the message she proclaims. It is not, however, a straightforward matter to 'read off' this evidence. The reason for this is the distorting effect of human sin, and of the fact that the created universe is under the curse. Scripture gives us reason to believe that, in the universe that was not cursed, the evidence of God's providential rule was much more apparent (Gn. 2:8–17). It also claims that, in the cursed creation, that evidence is much more scanty and ambiguous. It is not that, because of the curse upon the creation and the effect of human sin, God cannot 'get through', and is prevented from making his character known. Nor is it that, because of sin, he is less in control than he would be in a sinless universe. It is rather that part of the curse *is* just that ambiguity and distortion. For part of the curse consists in God withdrawing his goodness, and so, in this sense, leaving human beings to the consequences of their own folly (Rom. 1:24–32). But, in saying this, we are already trespassing into the second context of the doctrine of divine providence – providence in creation, fall and redemption. And so it is to this topic that we now turn.

4

PROVIDENCE IN CREATION, FALL AND REDEMPTION

The three different contexts in which we are considering divine providence – cosmic, ecclesiastic and personal – are like three different windows providing views of the one divine activity by which the world has been created and is being sustained and redeemed. In this chapter we shall be concerned with the second context – the need of reconciliation with God, and the provision of reconciliation through Christ.

It is an integral part of Christianity to maintain that this provision came in history. Christianity is not primarily an ethic (such as utilitarianism) or a philosophy (such as Platonism or Marxism). Nor have the events which the Christian celebrates been enacted in some super-historical realm far removed from everyday life. Redemption has been procured through the history of one nation, Israel, a history which culminated in the coming of Jesus Christ, in his ministry, death and resurrection, and in the life of the international Christian church which stems from that ministry.

In order to be able to think clearly about this aspect of divine providence, a number of preliminary issues need to be considered and to be kept in mind.

Preliminary

The overall aim in this book is to make an accurate study of God's activity now; and in this chapter, of God's activity now as it concerns the church. This can be done only by paying some attention to God's *former* providential activity in both the New Testament and Old Testament eras.

It is a fundamental fact of the Christian religion that the effects of God's providential activity have not been uniform throughout every period. It is not that God has exercised *less* providential control at some times than others, as if he were less interested or less in charge at these times. Rather, at some times his providential activity has had a particular public focus and interest. This fact is denied by those who hold, for whatever reason, that God's activity now must be the same as any earlier activity, that because miracles do not occur today it is not reasonable to believe that they occurred two thousand years ago.

Imagine Abraham, or David, or John the Baptist, or Matthew, each asking in their own time the question 'How is God active now?' The correct answer to such a question would be different in each case. God's providential activity at the time of Abraham was different from that at the time of David, and so on. In David's time, God governed the nation of Israel through detailed legislation absent in Abraham's time. God's presence was focused on the tabernacle worship. Different people were involved of course, but also *what* God did was different in each era, and perhaps even the kind of thing that he did was different too. If we are to come to some measure of understanding of how God is active now in the affairs of his church, then it is necessary to take into account what he has done in providence before now. For what he has done before makes what he does now clearer and more intelligible – though not perhaps fully intelligible. Biblical history is a narrative in which what went before helps to make sense of what comes after.

Our primary interest in this chapter is in the work of God in redemption. It would be misleading to imagine, however, that God's general providential work (as we might put it) is totally separate from his special providential activity as it relates to the church. It is a mistake to think that 'general' and 'special' are two labels for two separate boxes. This mistake is a serious one because it tempts us to draw the conclusion that God's world is in fact two worlds: the 'sacred' (having to do with redemption) and the 'secular' (having to do with everyday concerns). If the world is thought of in this way, it then becomes tempting to draw two further conclusions: that the sacred world is the world of our hearts and spirits, while the secular world is the world of our bodies; the sacred world is the world of Sunday, while the secular world is the world of Monday to Saturday; and so on.

But the Lord our God is one Lord, and the universe that he has created is one universe. It is therefore, more accurate to think of one providential order, the unfolding events of the one created universe, and of God having different purposes with respect to different parts or aspects of that one order.

The ship that carried Paul to Italy was like any other ship, and God's providential care upheld and directed its course as in the case of every other ship that sailed to Italy. Nevertheless, his purpose for that ship, or at least his purpose for one person and his friends in that ship, was inextricably tied up with the life and health of his church, and hence with the fulfilling of his redemptive purposes for humankind. His providential care extended to everyone on board, and life on board ship was the same for everyone; nevertheless, God's purposes for Paul and for his companions were, as far as we can tell, very different from those for the other passengers.

Another example may make this clearer. A Christian student or assembly-line worker functions more or less like any other student or assembly-line worker. God, in his providence, upholds him or her in that work just as he upholds those who deny God or curse him. But God's intention in upholding that Christian worker on the assembly line, is different from his intention with respect to others.

So the way to think of the relation of the church to the world is not to think of two boxes (not even two intersecting boxes), but rather to think of one providential order of amazing complexity within which God is working out different purposes for the different people within it.

How do we know that there are these different purposes?

By and large, we know it because of the fact that through his providence God has given us signs, evidence of these purposes. In particular, the history of Israel from the call of Abraham onwards is one set of signs that God has a separate, special intention for Abraham's children. To these signs can be added all the other known events in history through which redemption was procured, and then the ongoing life of the church and the remaking of individual men and women in their conversion to Christ. All these signs give evidence that, inseparably interwoven within God's general providence, is a special, redemptive care. There may be occasions when, for a time, that special providence works without public evidence. For example, unknown to Paul or to anyone else, Paul's early life, education and Pharisaism were a preparation not only for his call by grace (Gal. 1:15), but for the particular role he was to play in the early church as the apostle to the Gentiles. It is only when there are public signs of this providence that there is any chance of identifying God's special activity. But the absence of such signs ought not to lead us to think that the activity itself is absent.

The fall

The Christian faith is unintelligible without a fall. For at the heart of the faith is *redemption*, the restoring of humankind's relationship with God in a way which vindicates the righteousness of God and issues in men and women accepted in Christ and renewed in character. Restoration is possible only if men and women need restoring; and if they need restoration this can be only because there has been a lapse, or fall, from an original condition. Hence the fall is a necessary precondition of redemption. Scripture provides an account of the fall in the early chapters of Genesis, just as it describes Christ as the last Adam.

Provided that the fundamental point about the unintelligibility of the Christian religion without a fall is recognized, there is no need for us to become embroiled in discussion of the exact meaning of Genesis 3 or Romans 5. Was Genesis 3 historical? Were Adam and Eve real people? How does the biblical account in Genesis 3 square with modern science, and especially with the theory of evolution by natural selection? Is not the theory of evolution a theory of development and improvement, and not of a fall?

Happily, it is not necessary to become involved in these interesting and important, but difficult, questions, because in this study we are pursuing certain *systematic* enquiries. These enquiries concern the overall character of God's providential rule over his universe. Historical and exegetical details are of only secondary importance.

From a systematic point of view, there are, irrespective of the historical details, a limited number of logical possibilities of accounting for human sin. Either there was a fall or there was not. If there was a fall, then the exact details do not matter *from the point of view of considering God's providential rule over the fall*. If there was not a fall, then some other way of accounting for the entry of sin must be provided. This other way may or may not have distinctive implications for the doctrine of divine providence as it relates to human sin. On a non-fall account of human sin, for example, sin might be regarded as immaturity, even as the sort of immaturity for which a person is not responsible. Such a view of sin would have different implications for divine providence than if there was a fall in which humankind is culpable. We shall look at such a view when considering providence and evil in chapter 8.

Orthodox Christianity presupposes a fall, a 'historic' fall, one that really occurred. In what follows we shall take up this assumption without demur, and proceed to examine the consequences of the fall for divine providence. If readers have another understanding of the fall, then they will be able to make the necessary adjustments to the following account as we proceed.

Because Scripture provides us with no account of the fall other than the story of Adam and Eve, we shall conduct our discussion of the issues using that story. It ought to be stressed, though, that in doing this no detailed hermeneutical implications are being drawn. The question of the relation between the fall and scientific accounts of origins is being deliberately avoided and left open.

There is an important sense in which the fall affected the

creation, the natural order. For, according to the biblical account, death came as the (penal) consequence of the fall. When we examine nature, however, either at the common-sense level or with more scientific sophistication, it is clear that death, as a biological process, is now 'built into' the processes of nature. There are 'natural' processes of growth and decay of which it is possible to give a scientific account, and without which biochemistry would be radically different.

'Nature' can mean many different things. But in so far as death is now a built-in part of nature, there is a sense in which natural processes are unnatural, at least when considered from the vantage point of the creator who created all things good. The fall had wide, cosmic implications; it was not restricted to the human race, but the natural order was 'cursed' by the creator on account of human sin. The original story or drama, the story in which everything was 'very good', was revised in the light of human sin. Donald MacKay expressed this point in the following way:

> When an author decides to revise the story or drama he has conceived, it is clear that his revision is an act of *creation*, on a par with any of his earlier acts. 'Let us no longer have this, but that' is logically on the same footing as 'let there be this, and that'. The resulting created order, once again, is a spatio-temporal unity, whose whole past, present and future may therefore be expected to bear the marks of the revision.
>
> In discussion of the Genesis creation narrative it is often insufficiently realized that the last creative act is recorded not in chapters 1 and 2 but in chapter 3. 'And (God) said ... "Cursed is the ground because of you ... thorns and thistles it shall bring forth to you ..."' (verses 17–18 RSV). In short, we are told that the created order as we know it now is a *revised* version. Ours is *not the same drama* as that whose conception is narrated in chapters 1 and 2, and which God pronounced 'very good'. Some changes may for all we know have been slight; but in one

far-reaching respect our natural order is radically different: for ours is a creation 'under a curse', 'groaning in travail'. Not just its human history, but the very principles of natural law reflected in the growth of weeds, the toils of life and the inevitability of decay and death, are different from what they might have been, but for the fall.[1]

Orderliness

Despite the fall, the natural forces of the universe, and particularly of our planet, remain orderly. While the fall has resulted in the original creation being 'unmade', nevertheless, by the goodness of God, nature is largely predictable, at least at the 'micro' level even if not sub-atomically! God could have cursed the creation with much more disorderliness than we experience. Scripture appeals to this orderliness as evidence of God's faithfulness, and even represents it as a covenant promise (Gn. 8:22). But the orderliness is not so rigid as to preclude unexpected events, including miracles.

The orderliness in question extends beyond the physical regularity and reliability of the 'cursed' natural order to the operations of the human mind, to the functioning of reason, the management of affairs, and conscience. It includes the products of human ability and creativity, such as philosophy, science and technology, and culture, both popular and 'high'.

Theologians have used various ways of interpreting this orderliness. In the case of theologians in the 'natural law' tradition (usually those influenced by Thomas Aquinas, who was in turn influenced by Aristotle), the fall left 'nature' intact. On at least some interpretations of Aquinas, this means that humankind has a natural ability (*i.e.* one unaided by special, saving grace) to understand the moral law of God, and to arrive by reason and experience to the conclusion that God exists.

Others (such as those influenced by Abraham Kuyper, who was in turn building upon Calvin) have thought of such orderliness as evidence of God's common grace. The phrase 'common grace' is unfortunately ambiguous. In so far as it implies that the orderliness of the creation is sustained by the goodness of God, this certainly accords with scriptural teaching, and the thought expressed is not incompatible with a natural-law understanding. But the phrase may imply more, namely that God, in upholding what he does by his common grace, *approves* of what he upholds (*cf.* special grace, where such approval is obvious). But this does not follow. God may uphold what he does not approve of, and Scripture teaches that he does, as we shall see in more detail later. For this reason, others have wanted to understand this orderliness in terms of God's patience and his restraint of evil.

Besides being in itself an important feature of God's providential rule, knowledge of the predictability of nature adds to a person's responsibility. For knowing that we live in a predictable world, and not in one of complete chaos (if living in such a chaotic world could be imagined), we know that our actions will have more or less predictable consequences. Human activity is worthwhile because it takes place in a world that is so orderly that there is a reasonable chance of many plans and purposes being achieved.

It may at first glance seem to be a monstrous suggestion that the fall, which, as John Milton expressed it, 'brought death into the world and all our woe', was in accordance with the providence of God. But the consequences of supposing that it was not seem quite unacceptable.

Although there is no explicit and avowed teaching in Scripture that the fall was in accordance with the providence of God, there are two general reasons for supposing that it was. It is clear, as we have already seen, that the fall has a critical place in the divine purposes, for it is pivotal in the biblical message of salvation through Christ. Without the fall being presupposed, salvation is unnecessary and the announcement of salvation is unintelligible. For if there is no fall into sin, from what would we need to be saved? What would Christ's work have accomplished? Why would any incarnation have been necessary?

Further, we know from Scripture that God's providence extends to evil human acts. For example, Peter asserted that the crucifixion of Christ, the wicked act *par excellence*, was according to 'God's set purpose and foreknowledge' (Acts 2:23). From this we can learn that there is no reason in principle why the providence of God should not extend to all wicked and sinful actions. There can then be no reason in principle why the providence of God did not extend to the fall. There may, of course, be some special feature of the fall that would rule out God's providential interest in it. Given its importance, though, it is hard to imagine what that special feature could be. It is difficult to imagine that God could or would voluntarily surrender the superintendence of an act with such cataclysmic consequences, knowing what those consequences would be. There is therefore good reason to suppose that the fall was superintended by the providence of God.

In the preceding paragraphs two different expressions have been used to describe God's providence and the fall. It was said that the fall was 'in accordance with' the providence of God; and that it was 'superintended' by the providence of God. Let us, as summary shorthand for these expressions, use the word 'permit'. 'God permitted the fall' means, *at least*, that God knew that the fall was to occur and what its consequences would be. He upheld those involved in it when he could have *prevented* the fall.

'Permission' in the case of God is every bit as much an action as is 'performance'. People may give their permission through inadvertence or neglect or an unwillingness to take responsibility; but God cannot. His permission is 'willing permission', as Augustine expressed it. To say that God permitted the fall is thus to deny that he was ignorant of the fall before it occurred or that, knowing that it was to occur, he was powerless to prevent its occurrence. Whether God's permission of the fall, or indeed his permission of anything else, implies *more* than this is an important matter to be considered in chapter 8.

If it is correct to say that God permitted the fall, then with respect either to horrendous evils or to merest peccadilloes, it is also correct to say *at least* that God permits them to take place, in the sense of 'permit' that has been given. For, if God did not permit evil in this way, then both his knowledge and his power would be compromised. Events would occur that God did not know were going to occur; or, if he did know that they were going to occur but did not permit them, this

101

would be because he was powerless to prevent them. That is, in creating the universe God would have taken a substantial risk. And from the general biblical teaching about both God's knowledge and his power, these would be unacceptable conclusions to draw.

In saying this, we are leaving open the question of whether, according to Scripture, the evils which come as punishments for sin are themselves merely permitted by God, or whether God has a stronger relation to them. If God uses the sin of one person as the punishment of another, then this has obvious implications for God's relationship to that sin.

It is clear from Scripture that though it may be prudent (for reasons to be discussed later) to use the word 'permit' in the sense defined when referring to God's providential relation to sin and evil, God's providential relation to redemption is altogether more positive. He does not merely *permit* the redemption of men and women, nor does he merely provide *for* it; he *provides* it.

The covenant

It would obviously be impossible, in a work such as this, to plot in detail the way in which, according to Scripture, the providence of God is involved in the redemption of the church. All we can hope to do is to glance at a number of relevant biblical themes. Having considered these themes, we shall review a number of more general issues which arise today out of this second context. For these biblical themes provide an essential backcloth and support in answering the question, 'What is God doing now?'

Much of the character of God's redemptive involvement in human history is *covenantal*. That is to say, God unilaterally binds himself, by covenant promise, to act in certain ways. The way in which the regularity of nature has a covenantal character has already been noted.

The chief focus of the Old Testament, however, is in the establishing, by covenant, of a nation of God's own possession, from whom the Messiah would come. This is epitomized in the call of Abram from Ur of the Chaldeans, in the exodus of the children of Israel from the bondslavery of Egypt, and in the subsequent chequered history of Israel and Judah.

God's providence is seen at work in the history of Israel in different ways. In the case of God's special revelatory activity, in which he reveals his will to a person, or gives commands, the biblical account almost invariably presupposes that God is in charge of events. Thus, in the call of Abram, God's ability to keep his promises is assumed. So God's call to Abram, though something quite extraordinary, and making deep demands upon Abram's faith, is yet intelligible to Abram and something that he sees to be possible.

By his promises God binds himself and therefore (in providential terms) limits himself to the performance of certain actions in the future. Before the promises are made, there are no constraints; once they are made, God is bound by what he has said, and his providential activity has to be ordered accordingly. God is not bound by some external force, of course, but he binds himself. The necessity by which God is bound to keep his promises is not absolute necessity, the sort which makes 2 and 2 add up to 4; but a conditional necessity that arises out of the holy and all-powerful God having promised some particular thing. Having promised it, he is immutably committed to it, because he himself is immutable (Heb. 6:18, av).

Therefore, when God promises the land to Abram (Gn. 13:14–17), Scripture (and Abram) presuppose both God's right and his ability to grant the land to him. Not only that, but, since God promised the land to Abram, it becomes impossible for him to give it to anyone else. Hence the histories of other nations and families must be directed in such a way that God is able actually to bring his promise to pass. This is a general point, covering not only promises to Abram, but all promises and prophecies authentically made in the name of God. Such commitments limit God; but they also limit the action of others. For no course of action decided upon by a person can thwart God's purposes, even though at times God appears to change his mind (Gn. 6:7).

Another way in which the providence of God is seen emerges vividly in the events leading up to the marriage of Abraham's son, Isaac, to Rebekah, in Genesis 24. In sending his servant to look for a bride for Isaac, Abraham invoked both the promise of God and God's power to keep it. Further, in answer to the prayer of his servant (verse 12) God sends Rebekah in the precise way asked for by the servant, who acknowledges the leading of God in the matter (verse 27). This incident vividly illustrates a fundamental feature of the providence of God, that it is a *particular* providence, extending to the individual actions of particular people.

God does not, then, exercise providential control in a way that leaves two or more possible ways of achieving some goal. Nor does he will the end but leave the means to others. Nor is he concerned that history should simply exemplify certain general principles or morals or types of action. Rather, the providence of God is fine-grained; it extends to the occurrence of individual actions and to each aspect of each action.

Such particular providence is even more strikingly and dramatically seen in the career of Joseph: in his banishment to Egypt, his preservation and elevation there, and the way in which he was able to prepare for the flight of his family from Canaan. In this history there is a powerful instance of one feature of divine providence that assumes increasing importance as redemptive history unfolds. When they are safely in Egypt, and when their father, Jacob, is dead, Joseph's brothers ask for his forgiveness for the ill that they had done against him (Gn. 50:17). Joseph's reply was not only gracious but illuminating: 'You intended to harm me, but God intended it for good to accomplish what is now being done, the saving of many lives' (verse 20). That is, on Joseph's understanding God brought certain events to pass, events which had a beneficial end, and which were in accordance with his covenant promise to Abraham, using the evil intentions and actions of human beings. He does this, according to Joseph, without himself being implicated in the evil, and without diminishing in any way the evil of what was done to Joseph and the responsibility for that evil.

History

The covenantal framework, briefly illustrated here, provides an answer to the question, 'how did God's care for Israel differ from his care of other nations and groups living at the

104

same time?' For we must not imagine that his care for Israel or (in the New Testament) for the church is *exclusive*, or that in caring for his people God exercises no providential control over the remainder of his creation. For one thing, as we have seen, the history of Israel is dovetailed with the history of other nations.

A more detailed answer to the question is to be found in the fact that in creating a people 'for his own possession', God establishes certain ends or goals for them, which only they have. Part of the way in which the people of God are 'steered' towards those goals is by the way in which God establishes, in his promises, moral and spiritual parameters. Thus, if the people of God walk in humble obedience to his commands, blessing results; if they are disobedient and rebellious, they can expect chastisement and cursing.

The ebb and flow of Israel's history – the establishing of the kingdom and then its division, their being sent into exile, the return from captivity, and other similar events – may appear to be like the history of any other nation. Nevertheless, what happens to Israel has a distinctive ethical and spiritual justification, the fulfilment of their own distinctive role. This is absent from the histories of other nations.

Israel has a mission to the nations. The covenantal promise to Abraham, that in him and in his seed all nations of the earth will be blessed, finds its echo in David's response to God (2 Sa. 7:25f.; 1 Ki. 8:41–43). This connection between the success of the covenant and its impact upon the other nations is to be seen, for example, in Psalm 72. This prayer for the king asks (verse 17) that all nations will be blessed through him. And later, in Jeremiah's call to the people to return to the covenant and to honour its terms, the further connection is made that in doing so other nations will be blessed (Je. 4:2). It is by his word to king and to people through his prophets that the Lord brings a disobedient people to the fulfilment of their providentially appointed goal. In the next chapter we shall explore in more detail the place of such divine guidance in the fulfilling of providence.

What is true of Israel in the Old Testament is true of the Christian church in the New Testament era. The church is not a distinct national or political unit, and the life of

Christians and churches is socially and culturally intertwined with the lives of non-Christians. Nevertheless, God's purposes for them are distinct from his purposes for others. We shall look at this, and the problems that arise from it, later in this chapter, and in the next.

Miracles and prophecy

As we have already noted, miracles play an indispensable role in the biblical record of the providence of God towards his people. In forming a proper estimate of them in connection with God's providence, it is necessary to guard against a number of possible misunderstandings.

To begin with, it is important to note that the Bible does not employ a rigid distinction between the natural and the supernatural. Nor does it operate with a technical and precise definition of a miracle as a violation of, or suspension of a law of nature. Rather, 'signs and wonders' (some of which may have no scientific explanation) function as powerful expressions of God's power and grace. Their meaning is bound up with the meaning of the other events and teachings to which they point, and with which they are integrated. They do not have a scientific or magical significance of their own.

Moreover, miracles must not be regarded as divine tinkerings, as the way in which God deals with an emergency situation which has arisen unexpectedly. As we saw when discussing deism earlier, some philosophers and theologians have objected to the occurrence of miracles because they seemed to be dishonouring to God, as if the machinery of the universe were defective and God had to make running repairs. Whatever the shortcomings of this general approach, it quite correctly recognizes the inadequacy of supposing that miracles are needed because God's providential order is in danger of breaking down.

We may agree with Leibniz that God is perfect and that he does not do anything without having a sufficient reason to do it. It does not follow, however, that God cannot have a sufficient reason to perform a miracle; to act, that is, in a way that involves unprecedented changes in physical nature.

If miracles are not metaphysical first-aid, what are they?

They are *signs*, signs of God's grace, and of its urgency and power. They do not occur apart from the history of God's dealings with his people, but they are integral to that history. They invariably accompany new phases of God's redemptive activity, And their significance cannot be understood except in terms of the significance of the history of which they form a part.

As we have seen, the history of Israel and of the church is built upon covenantal promises which God fulfils by, among other things, providentially ordering the affairs of his people. The purpose of that history is to reveal God's grace in the redemption of men and women. Miracles are not signs of the power of God in the abstract, or magical tests of strength, or entertaining exhibitions of divine cleverness; but they are signs of grace. They are intended to make those who believe that God orders the affairs of nature for their good gasp – not only at the power of God in the miracle, but at power of a deeper magnitude in the revelation of saving grace which the miracles signal.

Redemptive grace is not a product of nature, but it is a direct and undeserved gift of God's love. It is not ordinary, but extraordinary. And what could better illustrate God's grace, as well as usher it forward, than actions of God which are unexpected and unparalleled? The miracles of the exodus, for example, are signs that God's redemption of his people from Israel is not a 'natural' occurrence, which could be paralleled with the histories of other nations; but that it is extraordinary, brought about by the direct, immediate, hand of God. And these miraculous activities are repeated not uniformly through the history of Israel, but at special times of awakening and revelation.

As we have already noted in connection with David and Jeremiah, the Lord also exercises his providential rule over Israel, enabling her to fulfil her destiny through 'my servants the prophets' (Je. 26:5). Their function is to call attention to the moral and spiritual failure of the people, to recall them to obedience and faithfulness to God and to a renewed dependence upon his mercy. It is in these ways, too, that the Lord providentially guides his people to their appointed destiny.

There is also a darker and more mysterious side to God's

providential direction of Israel. Not only does he form them by an extraordinary covenantal arrangement with Abraham, lead them into the promised land, miraculously deliver them from Egypt and reprimand them for disobedience through his prophets; he also chastens and reforms them when their unfaithfulness leads them to depart from him.

Thus the wilderness journey of forty years was an instance of the Lord chastening his people on account of their murmuring unbelief. The reason for this action was not petty vindictiveness on God's part, but a principled determination to uphold the terms of the original covenant. The covenant required trusting obedience, to which the people pledged themselves. When they lapsed into disobedience, this called forth the corrective action of God.

So not only is there fulfilment of the covenant, there is rebellion: in Abraham's choice of Hagar to be the mother of his son; in Jacob's usurping of Esau's birthright; in the rebellion of the children of Israel in the wilderness; in David's numbering of the people, and so on. Are not these acts of defiance and unbelief cases where God's purposes are thwarted and break down?

It may seem so. In order to examine this further, let us consider a number of these instances of defiance. We begin with God's repentance that he had chosen Israel, his resolve to destroy them and to form a new covenant people, and the intercession of Moses which brings about the Lord's change of mind (Ex. 32).

We have already commented upon the idea of the Lord's changing his mind when considering Calvin's view of divine accommodation. But if God does not really change his mind, was his initial threatening a *real* threatening? Was it genuine? How are we to decide the question? Presumably by attempting to establish what the Lord would have done had Moses not intervened. But it is extraordinarily difficult to establish the truth of many 'What if?' questions. Is there any reason to think that God would not have carried out his threat in those circumstances? Moses certainly believed the threat to be a real one. Did he have any grounds for believing that it was *not* genuine? Was not the threat warranted by the terms of the covenant? It was because Moses

108

took the threat seriously that he interceded.

In carrying out these purposes the Lord sometimes uses other human agencies, occasionally in surprising ways. In Isaiah 10 he refers to Sennacherib, the Assyrian king whom he was to send against his people, as 'the rod of my anger', (verse 5) a divinely chosen instrument of chastisement against a hypocritical nation. The Assyrian was used by the Lord to overcome his people and tread them down.

While the Assyrian was the Lord's 'rod', however, he himself had no inkling that he was performing this role ('But this is not what he intends'; verse 7). The Assyrian's intention was not to act as a divine chastiser, but to plunder Israel and other nations for his own ends in a high-handed and imperious way. Because of this, when he has carried out what the Lord intends against Israel, then he in turn will be punished for his evil.

In a similar vein Cyrus is referred to as the 'shepherd' of God and, even more extraordinarily, as his 'anointed' (Is. 44:28; 45:1) whose right hand is held by the Lord. He is sent to subdue the nations for 'the sake of Jacob my servant' even though he does not know the Lord (45:45). Both these occasions illustrate the principle that 'The king's heart is in the hand of the LORD; he directs it like a watercourse wherever he pleases' (Pr. 21:1). As suggested earlier, one way of thinking of these occurrences is in terms of a hierarchy of causes, with God as the primary cause, and men and women as the secondary causes. We shall consider this idea in greater detail later on.

Whether it is chastening or deliverance, the teaching is clearly that the Lord uses instruments who, in fulfilling their own plans, are also fulfilling his. As with Joseph and his brothers, the Lord is able to use his creatures without either detracting from the evil of their intentions, nor contaminating himself by such use.

The incarnation

This all too brief allusion to the Old Testament history shows that no sharp distinction can be made between the providence of God and his grace. Biblical religion is a historical religion, not a set of abstract ideals or ethical teachings. Redemption is achieved through God's activity in history. It is not possible to say that 'providence' covers 'everyday' occurrences and 'grace' the rest. Providence is frequently gracious, and grace is invariably providential in character.

For the Christian, the providence of God in history is seen supremely and uniquely in the incarnation, ministry, death and resurrection of Christ. It is Christ of whom the prophets spoke: God is himself, in the person of his Son 'contracted' (as Charles Wesley put it) to the human form of a servant, living within the confines of history. The fact of the incarnation is thus the supreme act of divine providence.

It would be possible to dwell on the exact meaning of 'the fulness of the time', and on the details associated with the birth of Jesus Christ at Bethlehem. The harsh truth is, however, that God the Son does not become incarnate to 'take charge', but to subject himself to bodily weakness and human wickedness. The emphasis, in the incarnation, is not on the God providing *for* Christ (though there is this aspect), but rather on Christ as the divine provision for others.

The long-expected and long-promised Messiah comes in a form that surprises and offends, and submits himself not only to bodily weakness and limitation, but to indignity and evil. The basic, controlling providential principle lying behind the incarnation and ministry of Christ was announced by Peter on the day of Pentecost:

> This man was handed over to you by God's set purpose and foreknowledge; and you, with the help of wicked men, put him to death by nailing him to the cross. But God raised him from the dead, freeing him from the agony of death, because it was impossible for death to keep its hand on him (Acts 2:23–24).

The rebellious nature of the children of Israel, to which we have referred earlier, reaches its climax in the crucifixion of Christ.

The death of Christ was no more an 'accident' than the incarnation. It is inaccurate to portray the events of Calvary as if wicked men had thwarted Christ's own purposes. He had long known those purposes. He was aware that it was his Father's work that he came to do, that he had a baptism with which to be baptized. He recognized at Caesarea Philippi the fate that lay in store for him, that he must go up to Jerusalem to suffer, to die and to be raised from the dead (Mt. 16:21). It is to this divinely appointed goal that he steadfastly set his face.

So once again, in the most dramatic and central fashion, the same mysterious providential arrangement obtains here as in such cases as that of Joseph and his brothers, and of Sennacherib and Cyrus. The Lord uses wicked people to further his purpose. Evil people crucify Christ. Yet such crucifixion is not fortuitous, nor a mere human tragedy, but it is by the determinate counsel and foreknowledge of God. The Lord did not conspire with these wicked people; nonetheless he used their wickedness for his own pure ends.

The dramatic difference in the case of the crucifixion is that in the sequel, with no human agency, the Lord himself is raised from the dead by the power of God. To Christ all power and authority are given, and he ascends to his Father in a glorified and triumphant form.

So at the heart of the Christian faith is an act of evil perpetrated against the Son of God. Difficult though it may be for us to grasp, the greatest act of evil was not a horrendous human tragedy, such as a concentration camp or an earthquake, but the putting to death of God's Messiah. It is necessary for the Christian to bear this fact in mind when thinking about the relationship between providence and evil, as we shall try to do in chapter 8.

Old Testament attitudes

So far in this chapter we have briefly glanced at features of the biblical history to provide one important – in many ways the most important – aspect of the teaching of Scripture on providence. But the richness of Scripture is such that there are other almost equally important and complementary, aspects to the teaching that we must now notice. These have to do not with God's providence so much as with human attitudes to it.

In the Old Testament, as one might expect, there is a variety of attitudes to the workings of divine providence. Men and women frequently rejoice when things appear to go well with them, and complain when they do not. But there are also more distinctive attitudes brought about by a recognition of the working of that providence itself. For the idea of God's rule over them was a consciously operating principle in the lives of many Old Testament men and women.

One of the distinctive features of Old Testament piety is the recognition, on the part of certain people, that the Lord has the right to do with their lives what he has done. This is seen most vividly and memorably in the case of Job who, having lost almost everything at the hands of the Lord, recognizes that God is the sovereign, possessing the right to give or to withhold as he sees fit:

> 'The LORD gave and the LORD has taken away;
>   may the name of the Lord be praised' (Jb. 1:21).

> 'Shall we accept good from God, and not trouble?'
> (Jb. 2:10).

Such an attitude may seem to be fatalistic, but it is not. Its expression does not prevent Job from agonizing with God about what has happened to him. Nevertheless, it is a recognition by Job of God's right to deal with him, and the basis of this is Job's belief that his life is controlled by God himself. For this reason he is able to trust God no matter what the consequences.

A similar attitude in different circumstances is expressed by Habakkuk the prophet, who is able to say that even

> Though the fig-tree does not bud
>   and there are no grapes on the vines,
> though the olive crop fails
>   and the fields produce no food,
> though there are no sheep in the pen
>   and no cattle in the stalls,
> yet I will rejoice in the LORD,
>   I will be joyful in God my Saviour (Hab. 3:17–18).

Habakkuk, like Job, did not proportion his faith to the degree to which he received the outward evidences of divine favour and blessing, though blessings had been promised to Israel in so far as the nation remained faithful to the covenant.

A third type of case is where an individual accepts the judgment of God upon himself. David recognized this in the premature death of his and Bathsheba's child, even though he prayed for the child's recovery (2 Sa. 12:7–14). Perhaps a clearer example of such acceptance is that of Eli. When told by Samuel that his house would be judged because of the wickedness of his sons, Eli responded, 'He is the Lord; let him do what is good in his eyes' (1 Sa. 3:18).

A final example is a rather different case. There were occasions when individuals complained to God about the apparent injustice or unfairness of his providence. A classic example is Psalm 73, where Asaph expresses his perplexity at the prosperity of the wicked, the ungodly who prosper in the world (verse 12). This perplexity is expressed more generally in the thought of the Teacher (Ec. 9:2). Asaph's perplexity is resolved only when he comes to recognize that the prosperity in quesiton is temporary, and only a prelude to their destruction (verses 17–18).

What all these different attitudes have in common is that they refer perplexity, distress, or personal setback to the will of God. The people in question are able to do this only because of their conviction that, as his covenant people, the Lord governs all their affairs. They recognize that wicked people and acts of judgment and chastisement, as well as days of prosperity and blessing, were in the hands of the Lord and that they came their way in accordance with divine wisdom. They drew this conviction, no doubt, not only from the history of Israel, but also from the teaching of prophets (as we have seen) and from statements such as those in the wisdom literature which we have already noted. The Lord has the hearts of kings in his hands; he determines the outcome of even seemingly chance events such as the drawing of a lot (Pr. 16:33). There is thus a strong link in the Old Testament between convictions about the scope and depth of divine providence and the development of faith and piety.

New Testament attitudes

The great theological difference between the Testaments is, of course, that in the New Testament era Christ has vanquished sin and has been raised triumphant. To him has been granted all power and authority. Despite this, there are important elements of continuity between the Old and New Testaments. Having looked at the part played by providence in the incarnation and ministry of Christ, we shall concentrate now on personal attitudes to the ways of God, noting some similarities in these to those of the Old Testament characters which were considered in the last section.

Any sketch of New Testament attitudes to providence must begin with Christ's teaching to his disciples about their need to be free from care and anxiety. The reason for such freedom, according to Christ, should be the knowledge that God providentially cares for them. He knows their needs; the hairs of their heads are all numbered; they are of more value than many sparrows; it is the Father's good pleasure to give them the kingdom (Lk. 12:7, 22–32).

One prominent instance is Paul's response to his 'thorn in the flesh' (2 Cor. 12:7). He exhibits an attitude of resignation to the divine will, once that will has been definitively made known to him. Paul recognizes that the providence of God is sometimes unpleasant, but that behind the pain there is a wider purpose. This personal attitude of Paul's is echoed and supported by more general teaching about the significance and purpose of chastisement (*e.g.* Heb. 12).

There are also more general statements, such as that in the letter of James:

> Now listen, you who say, 'Today or tomorrow we will go to this or that city, spend a year there, carry on business and make money.' Why, you do not even know what will happen tomorrow. What is your life? You are a mist that appears for a little while and then vanishes. Instead you ought to say, 'If it is the Lord's will, we will live and do this or that' (Jas. 4:13–15).

Here James reminds his readers that they cannot take tomorrow for granted; not because of fate, or luck, or even human weakness (although that thought is prominent in the passage). Rather, the implication is that whether or not such weakness leads to an inability to do what one wants to do is entirely a matter of the will of God. A recognition of the will of God, therefore, should preface all one's plans.

But by far the most comprehensive statement of divine providence as it affects both the individual Christian and the church is that of Paul in Romans 8:

> And we know that in all things God works for the good of those who love him, who have been called according to his purpose. For those God foreknew he also predestined to be conformed to the likeness of his Son, that he might be the firstborn among many brothers. And those he predestined, he also called; those he called, he also justified; those he justified, he also glorified (Rom. 8:28–30).

This statement occurs in a context in which Paul recognizes the importance of the fact that Christians are called to suffer with Christ as part of their believing union with him. As a believer, a person is united to Christ in his suffering, crucifixion and resurrection. And so Paul stresses that providential suffering is what believers are to expect as part of their joint-heirship with Christ (Rom. 8:17). This does not mean that believers' sufferings are expiatory, but they are an inevitable part of that obedient following of Christ to which each believer is called (*cf*. Jn. 15:18–19). Suffering as a Christian has an evangelical character, and an evangelical justification (1 Pet. 4:16).

Paul is not saying that all those who love God will get everything that they want; or that they will be happy; or that it is not possible for them to think of how they might, on one particular occasion, have been happier or more fulfilled than they were. It is clear from the passage that the 'good' is given a distinctive characterization, equivalent to 'conformity to the likeness of his Son', Christ. What Paul is saying is that the lives of those who love God are ordered by God for the

115

purpose of conforming them to Christ's image, to the moral and spiritual character of Christ.

What are the 'all things' to which Paul refers? What are his readers led to expect by these words? Paul states that neither 'trouble or hardship or persecution or famine or nakedness or danger or sword' (Rom. 8:35), can separate the lover of God from the love of Christ. So if trouble, say, should dog the path of a lover of God, then that person may draw at least two conclusions. One is that the trouble is sent by God; it does not occur by accident or chance. The second conclusion is that the arrival of the trouble, or whatever it might be, is purposive, even though it may not be possible to detect its exact purpose. It is one of the 'all things' which work together for the good of the individual concerned, for the believer's conformity to Christ's character.

It might seem that Paul's teaching here is likely to produce fatalism in his hearers. If the events of life as they unfold inevitably lead to their conformity to Christ, what need they care? What possible responsibility do they have in this situation?

But this would be to forget that Paul is writing 'to those who love' God. They are not passive or fatalistic in character. Their desire is to please God by keeping his commands, which is the test and measure of their love. In so far as they are consistent, they will wish to use each of the 'all things' which come their way to express their love and obedience to God. We shall consider in the next chapter the place that obedience to God has in the way in which God guides his people.

The statement that Paul is making about all things working together for good is thus not an *unconditional* statement. It does not hold no matter what. In making it Paul assumes the fulfilling of certain other conditions. Notably, he makes the assumption that the lover of God will desire to please God by obeying him. All things therefore work together for good, not *exclusively* of any attitude that the believer might take up, but inclusive of his other obedience. Indeed, part of the reason for Paul's writing this passage is, presumably, to inculcate such obedient and trustful attitudes on the part of the lovers of God, to fortify them in their obedience in a world of setbacks and peril.

One of the striking consequences of Paul's view is the possibility that there is nothing in the events that befall a lover of God to distinguish him from someone who is not in that position. As we noted earlier, the Teacher claimed that 'all share a common destiny' (Ec. 9:2), and this is true of life in general. Some who are godly prosper, while some starve; some ungodly prosper, while some starve; and so on. There is then a clear sense in which Paul envisages God being a 'hidden' God; in the midst of the trials and setbacks of life there may be no clear evidence, given those setbacks alone, that God loves the person. We shall take up this important matter shortly, when considering personal guidance.

Is it, therefore, either meaningless or irrational to love God in these circumstances? It is neither of these things, according to Paul, since the believers' attitude to God is grounded not only in what may happen to them from day to day, but chiefly in the overall significance of what is happening to them, in what those events *mean*. And their significance is to be found both in what has happened in the past (in conversion to God) and in what will happen to them in the future (the consummation of all things in the vision of God). The attitude to God of those who love him is now, or ought to be, rooted in the significance of God's activity in the past, and in his promised activity in the future.

Is the world for the church?

The discussion just completed raises an interesting and acute question. As we have noted, Paul's statement about divine providence as it affects the prospects of the believer is all-embracing. *All things* work together for good. They work together for the good of the Christians, and for the good of the church. This has staggering implications. It means that everything that occurs is for the benefit of some – namely, of the church. Does Paul mean that those who are not the church do not benefit at all?

It would be an ill-drawn caricature to suppose that Paul is teaching that no-one benefits from anything that happens except the Christians. Obviously this is false. If a sewer is dug, then those who use the sewer benefit from it, whoever they may be. Nor is Paul arguing that there is nothing that is worth while in itself. His argument does not touch the person who argues that education, or art, or hill-walking, or plant-breeding, or whatever it might be, is a worthwhile end in itself, needing no extrinsic justification, no justification in terms of any other end or ends.

Paul is concerned not about ends, or about worthwhileness, but about *ultimate* ends and *ultimate* worthwhileness. He is saying that in the case of the Christian, even the most tedious or heart-rending circumstance, because God has providentially arranged it in accordance with his wisdom, will work together with all other circumstances for the Christian's good (in the tacitly conditional manner sketched earlier).

Given that Paul is writing about what is for the *ultimate* benefit of the lover of God, then what he is saying is that all things, including those matters which people regard as worth while (and worthless) in themselves, work together for the benefit of the Christian church. In this sense the world is for the church.

The paradox of what Paul is saying can be lessened further by considering that at any one point in history it is not clear who are the church and who are the world. No doubt ultimately this will be clear, but it is not clear yet. It is not clear, for example, which of those who are not yet lovers of God may still become such.

If we think of all that happens as 'history', then the Christian idea of providence may be said to give us the rudiments of a philosophy of history. For as providence has a course, so does history – not only the history of redemption but the history of the entire human civilization. To say this, though, is not to say either that theologians have, or anyone else has, the interpretative key to history that will, in Spengler or Toynbee fashion, enable them to predict its course, even in outline. The record of those who have attempted such feats of prophecy is not an enviable one.

Nor does such an attitude to history imply that there is any historical method other than a patient unearthing of the facts of the past. But it does imply a teleological view of history, even though the *telos* is found outside history, in the purpose of God. The fact of the inscrutability of God's purposes does not mean that human actions have no value or significance. Far from it; they have significance because they are the actions of those who are made in the image of God, and their actions have significance precisely because they contribute uniquely to the meaning of the whole.

Providence and grace

When a person becomes a lover of God, how is that to be explained? Is it sufficient to say that the explanation lies in the events of providence alone? Is conversion to God explicable solely in terms of a special coming together of the events of providence, or is there more? Put differently, can conversion be explained naturalistically, or is there the equivalent of a miracle in each conversion?

We have seen that it is impossible to separate the events of providence from those of God's redemption, since redemption occurs in history in accordance with the plan of God. Certainly it is unwise to attempt to equate 'providence' with 'common grace' as some have done. For while providence includes common grace, it also embraces the events of God's special grace in redemptive history. Providence includes predestination.

These remarks apply also to the more subjective or personal aspects of redemption. For as we have asked how extensive the scope of divine providence is, so we may ask how *intensive* it is. Scripture portrays God as the one from whom no secrets are hidden. Psalm 139 goes into great and eloquent detail about this. And, as we have already seen, God has the hearts of kings in his hands; how much more the hearts of the kings' subjects! In a way which is entirely consistent with this, the Lord is portrayed not only as providing redemption through the works of God in history, but also as *effecting* that redemption in the lives of men and women. So when Paul states that God is at work in the lives of his children, both 'to will and to act according to his good purpose' (Phil. 2:13), he is expressing the view that God effects faith and Christian virtue in the characters of his people. In this he is echoing Christ's teaching about the new birth (Jn. 3).

119

On a 'risk' view of providence of the sort sketched earlier, there is no way in which God can providentially ensure that any particular person becomes a Christian. Whether or not that happens would depend upon the free choice of the person in question. But on the view we have favoured and developed, the 'no-risk' view, God can so order the events of a persons's life as to ensure that he or she becomes a Christian. Paul seems to endorse this view when he writes of God separating him from his mother's womb and calling him by his grace (Gal. 1:15). It is as if the two great focal points, birth and second birth, are linked by one chain of divine providence.

There are difficulties with this view, of course. For just as some object to the 'no-risk' view of providence on the grounds that it makes God the author of sin, so some take particular exception to the idea of God's effective grace, on the grounds that it makes a person a puppet whom God manipulates for his own ends. We shall explore these difficulties at length in chapter 7. It is perhaps a sufficient response at present to note that the provision of such effective grace is portrayed in Scripture as a *rescue* of someone who cannot rescue himself. Further, the provision of such grace, far from making a person into a puppet, actually frees him, making a puppet into a person.

5

PROVIDENCE
AND GUIDANCE

We are studying God's providence in terms of three separate but related contexts in which issues can arise about God's activity now. The previous two chapters sketched two of these contexts. Each of these is, of necessity, somewhat general and impersonal.

In this chapter we shall be concerned with the much more specific and immediate question of how divine providence affects the life of the Christian. This has two parts: the first concerns how the Christian, who recognizes and accepts the fact of divine providence, is to live in the light of it. What operational consequences is the fact of divine providence, as established in the first two contexts, to have for the Christian? The second has to do with the effect of God's activity now upon the Christian, even if he or she does not recognize divine providence for what it is.

While these questions are more concrete and personal than those we have been dealing with, they can be satisfactorily addressed only if the other two frameworks of understanding are kept in mind. Christians' understanding of how divine providence affects them should build on their awareness of

God's providence as it is exercised both upon the world at large, and upon the church.

Yet it is obvious that while the *fact* that God providentially guides the Christian can be deduced from the fact that he guides the church (for the Christian is a member of the church), *how* he guides cannot be deduced. For Christians have only to glance around them, or to have the faintest inkling of the history of the church, to see that the circumstances of Christians differ markedly. It is thus quite implausible to suppose that there is one uniform pattern of providential guidance for every Christian. So how do we get from the rather general truths about divine providence to the often acute and difficult problems – unique to his or her circumstances – encountered by the Christian?

This question divides into two. First, how do Christians *recognize* divine providence in their lives? Granted that the hand of God is on them, what points does that hand become visible? Does it ever become visible? Secondly, how can Christians align themselves with divine providence in the future so as to be in harmony with the divine purpose?

Discerning the pattern

As we have stressed, if we take the scriptural view that all events fall under the control of divine providence, then the word 'providence' becomes a synonym for 'whatever happens'. Then the question how Christians recognize the hand of God is quickly answered. Whatever happens to Christians is providential, because everything that happens to anyone is providential. If they trip over the kerb, or see a sunset, or get married, or fall ill, then each of these events is providential. If everything that happens is providential then the 'pattern' (such as it is) is formed by that totality of events. On this understanding of the word, 'providence' is a purely *descriptive* term; it describes what happens, all that happens and only what happens.

Even if by the term 'divine providence' were meant not everything that happens but only some of the things that happen, the same point would hold. 'Providence' describes those events; though, if divine providence were concerned with only some events, there would be the additional problem of how to identify the set of events which is providential from the remaining events which are not.

This descriptive sense is of enormous importance in understanding divine providence as it affects the individual Christian, and we shall return to it. It is not *this* sense of providence, however, that is in mind when Christians are exercised by the need to discern God's guidance. What they want to know is how to ensure that the particular events of their lives form a pattern, so that from recognizing that pattern they can be assured that God is guiding them. Here it is not 'providence' as a *descriptive* term that is in view, but as a *normative* or *evaluative* term.

For Christians, understandably enough, wish to know that they are being benefited by all the events of their lives, all of which are under divine providence. They also wish to know *how* they are being benefited. 'Providence', in such a context, then becomes an evaluation word. For an event to be described as 'providential', in this evaluative sense, does not merely signify that the event took place, but that the event that took place was in some identifiable sense productive of good for the person concerned, or that it will be. When people use the word 'providential', it is this idea of providence as beneficial that they usually have in mind.

Let us try to start answering this question by isolating some of the ways in which Christians do in fact use the word 'providential' in this evaluative sense.

Suppose that 'flu is widespread and yet, despite the fact that all the members of her family go down with it, Mrs Smith does not. She took all reasonable precautions against contracting the illness and regards the fact that she was spared the 'flu as 'providential', as a blessing from God, an instance of his goodness. What she means by this is at least the following: her not going down with 'flu is a good thing and it was God that prevented her going down with 'flu. (This case, and some of the others we shall shortly consider, raises problems about those who *did* go down with 'flu. We shall try to consider these difficulties, however, when dealing with providence and evil in chapter 8.)

Imagine that Mr Jones, while joining the motorway from a

slip-road, fails to look into his rear-view mirror and narrowly avoids an accident only because another car brakes hard to avoid him. Unlike Mrs Smith, who took reasonable precautions against getting 'flu, Mr Jones was careless. There was no reason why, as far as his own performance was concerned, the accident ought not to have happened; and yet it did not happen. When he arrives home he says that it was 'providential' that he was not involved in a serious motorway accident. What he means by this is that God in his goodness overruled or compensated for his carelessness so as to bring about a beneficial effect: his safe arrival home.

Suppose that Mr Robinson, a struggling salesman, having missed his train, finds himself standing on the platform next to an old school friend. They get talking, and as a result, the old friend (who turns out to be a successful businessman) places a large order for Mr Robinson's products. Mr Robinson says, not unreasonably, that if he had caught the train which he planned to catch, and which he usually caught, he would not have gained this business. On reflection, he says that is was 'providential' that he missed the train. What he means by this is at least the following: that the circumstances were unplanned, that there was an unforeseen and unintended disproportion between what led to the outcome and the outcome itself; and that the outcome was beneficial to him.

These are not the only sorts of events which justify the description 'providential' in its evaluative sense. For one thing, there is a special set of such events which are regarded as answers to prayer. An attempt will be made to examine the relation of prayer to providence in chapter 6. But all the events so far described contain two features: there is an element of unexpectedness or undeservedness or disproportion about the events, and the outcome of the events is believed to be a benefit of some kind to the person concerned.

Let us call such events as these cases of *immediate providence*. Immediate providence provides one level at which it is possible to discern a pattern in events, a pattern which justifies calling those events providential. But the very fact that these are cases of immediate providence means that they are liable to further judgment and refinement by the person concerned, in the light of continuing experience. There are two reasons why this further assessment might be required.

Even the most elementary events of human life can have innumerable consequences, some of which may be quite important. It may be that, as the further consequences of the events unfold and come to be known, the person who at one stage described them as 'providential', in the positively evaluative sense, may be reluctant to continue to do so. For it may be that what once appeared to be a beneficial outcome is seen now to be part of a wider picture whose outcome, on balance, is judged to be non-beneficial. Let us call providence in this sense *retrospective providence*.

An example of retrospective providence might be the following development of an earlier example. As a result of the increased sales, Mr Robinson is tempted to expand his business. This results in overexpansion and he becomes bankrupt. In these circumstances, he will naturally enough be less ready to say that what happened on the platform after he missed his train was 'providential', in the positively evaluative sense. He may continue to do so, however, depending on how he regards the later events.

Another reason why a further assessment of the pattern of events might be called for has to do with the discussion in the last chapter. There we saw that the overarching principle, as far as the Christian church is concerned, is the Pauline assurance that all things work together for the good of those who love God, where by 'the good' is meant conformity to the image of Christ.

It might be a relatively easy thing, for all but the deepest pessimist, provisionally to discern a good outcome in a particular pattern of events. It is much less easy to recognize that particular events have a special or an unusual part to play in helping to conform a Christian to the image of Christ, that is, to work to his good in the sense of Romans 8:28. An event which is regarded as providential in the sense already discussed in the examples might be regarded as contributing no more to conforming a person to the image of God than any other event. Perhaps setbacks, heartache or bodily weakness will, in a particular case, contribute more.

There are a number of reasons for being hesitant about

coming to a conclusion on how some particular event contributes to the development of the image of Christ in a person. One reason is that what conformity to the image of Christ means is rather vague and indeterminate. It implies certain ethical and spiritual ideals, but what that mix of those ideals is in the case of any one particular individual is far from clear. Further, a person may be deficient in the degree of self-knowledge required in order to assess a particular event in terms of its spiritually or morally beneficial effects. In a parallel fashion, think of how difficult it is to say in what precise ways particular events help to form character. For a variety of reasons it may be that other people are the better judges. In any case, an event does not have to be judged beneficially providential at the time it occurs for it to be so.

There are other reasons that caution against passing such judgments on the significance of particular events. One reason is that, according to Scripture, the time-scale for a person being conformed to the image of Christ is the whole of that person's life. Any judgment about the significance of one event, or series of events, should therefore be appropriately tentative and open to revision in the light of subsequent experience.

The Bible does not, it seems, promise that a person's life will form a discernible pattern, with a beginning, a middle and an end. Many lives are completely patternless or marked by tragedy; early promise may be cut off by serious illness or death. It would be completely false to Scripture to suppose that in order for people to be assured that the events of their lives are ordered by providence for a good end, they should be able to discern some overall pattern or 'story' in their lives. The pressing need to discern such a pattern can often lead to unnecessary frustration and heartache.

We can see from this how mistaken and misguided are those who teach that a well-ordered Christian life will be a *happy* life, or a *long* life, or a *prosperous* life or a *healthy* life. A survey of the lives of the saintliest of the people of God provides no confirmation of such claims. There are no promises of God which guarantee any of this; and in fact there are teachings of Scripture which suggest that it is impossible to discern a pattern to the lives of believers.

According to Scripture *all* events that affect a person's life have value: 'In *all things* God works for the good . . .' Not until all the events of a person's life have occurred, until that life has come to an end, could the contributory significance of any particular event or events be definitely assessed. In this sense, the meaning of a life lies outside that life.

Tentativeness in passing a verdict upon what happens is further underlined by another fact. If all events are embraced by divine providence, and all events work together for the Christian's good, then even the Christian's sins work together for his or her good: not so much the sins *as* sins, but what arises out of them; what they may, in the providence of God, lead to; and what a Christian may learn from being made aware of them. A Christian naturally will be very reluctant indeed to say what may be the positive significance of some particular shameful episode. The events may be so difficult to cope with that there may be a reluctance even to think about them. Perhaps the event was too painful to dwell upon, the emotions too aroused to obtain a clear view, and so on.

The argument so far can be summed up in the following way. There is an obvious sense in which a person may say of a particular event that it is providential. But the significance of that event, and of any other events, will inevitably be modified in the light of what follows. A person should be correspondingly tentative in saying of some particular event that it was in a marked or special sense providential (while bearing in mind that Scripture teaches that all events are providential). Any discerned pattern, however tentative, is going to be retrospective.

But what if no pattern at all can be discerned? What if a life, a Christian life even, seems marked by pointlessness and tragedy? What if whole stretches of a life are stamped by monotony, or by loss and adversity? The sense of these difficulties may be so overwhelming as to prevent a person thinking calmly or rationally about his or her life as a whole. What then? It is at this point that the wider framework of understanding discussed in the last chapter should receive emphasis. A recognition of divine providence might, in these circumstances, depend upon faith holding on to the fact of this framework when there is nothing else. This is the experience foreshadowed by Habakkuk, and by Job's 'Though he slay me, yet will I hope in him' (Jb. 13:15). Such words must have formed the substance of the faith in God of many a martyr and hero of the faith.

In such situations God may seem hostile, or indifferent to their fate, at least as measured by their estimate of the events of their lives. Is this a reason for them to conclude that God is not providing? In practice this is what often happens. To prevent this, an attempt should be made to invoke those more basic frameworks of understanding that we have been considering in the earlier chapters: the fact that God upholds all events that take place, and is in control of them in virtue of the fact that he is creator and Lord of all. More especially, in virtue of his covenant promise ratified in the blood of Christ, God is working every event together for the good of the believers, even when they cannot see this.

Even if Christians can discern no overall meaning to their lives, or to any part of them, it would be unwarranted to conclude from this that all things are not working together for their good.

Throughout this discussion we have stressed that recognizing divine providence is a difficult and tentative business. The best hope of doing so is to look back over our lives from some distance, with the Bible as our interpreter. The recognition of providence is retrospective. But such caution, even scepticism, does not mean that whether or not an event is providential is simply a matter of taste or of one's point of view.

Rather, the tentativeness or scepticism reflects the fact that as human beings we do not have sufficient data to make definitive judgments on the significance of the events in our lives. Nor are we free from bias. Any attempt to demonstrate the significance that our lives have, or to construct a definitive narrative out of the events of our lives, must be provisional. But such tentativeness is not simply the view that nothing makes an event providential except its being perceived as such. It means the precise opposite of this. Often Christians are left to affirm that their lives are governed by divine providence while lacking the data to demonstrate this. This is part of the trial of their faith.

Providence is invoked not only when explanations of what happens are lacking, but also when they are available but are not, by themselves, sufficient. The explanation of why a person missed an appointment might be perfectly straightforward: because of heavy traffic. At one level, this answer is quite sufficient and satisfactory. Nevertheless, in affirming that missing the appointment was providential, the Christian is appealing to a higher explanatory framework, one that does not invalidate the lower-level explanation but incorporates it.

So far, we have thought of providence as being a matter of interpreting the present and past events of one's life within a framework. Is there any place for the interpretation of a life *pro*spectively? Is it possible to anticipate the course of divine providence? At first glance it may seem that it is, for Scripture teaches that the providence of God is not bounded by the past and the present, but extends to the future. God knows the end from the beginning. Not only that; Scripture teaches that from time to time God has empowered his prophets to foretell what will come to pass. And Christ knew in some detail how he would die. So there is no difficulty in *principle* about foretelling the future.

Despite this, Scripture teaches that there is no reason to think that we can anticipate or predict what will happen to us tomorrow or the next day. Certain individuals, such as Hezekiah, may have received a special promise or warrant from God. There is no basis for thinking, however, that we may be given some special insight, or that we are to expect some intimation from God on the subject. Indeed, the teaching of Scripture is entirely the other way. The Bible stresses that none of us knows what a day may bring forth, and that our lives cannot be planned definitively but are subject to the will of God. Any other attitude is unwarranted, and verges on the blasphemous, for by it we presume to take into our own hands matters which God keeps in his.

Of course, a person may be able to give probable estimates to events. If one could not do this – if any event was as likely to occur as any other event – then it would be impossible to plan or to think rationally about the future. We believe that our children will, in all likelihood, outlive us. We know that we shall die. But we cannot be certain that our children will

129

outlive us, and we cannot (unless we resolve to end our lives ourselves) know very far in advance either the time or the manner of our death. Yet the providence of God extends over all events, past, present and future.

Guidance

It cannot be denied that the pressure on some people to know what is going to happen to them can sometimes be very great. For such people the fact that the future is hidden represents an unwelcome barrier which they would dearly like to break down. In effect, they hope to know the future in order to allay the anxieties of the present. For all they know to the contrary, though, being made aware of the future might add to those anxieties!

The providence of God as it affects the future raises the whole topic of the relationship between providence and guidance. This frequently arouses intense concern among Christians, and some confusion. Both the concern and the confusion arise from the feeling that one advantage of belief in divine providence is that the future has a determinate outcome known and willed by God. If only the 'will of God' could be discerned, then it would be possible to 'tap into' divine providence, to align one's own life to the life of God, and so live out one's life in a fulfilling and satisfactory manner.

There is no doubt that the providence of God does have important consequences for personal guidance. But unfortunately an attitude such as that just sketched betokens a number of confusions. It is necessary to say something about these before looking more positively at the way in which divine providence and personal guidance come together.

How does divine providence guide? How can divine providence guide? As we have seen, there is a sense in which, since all that happens is under the control of God, all that happens is under his guidance. Nevertheless, the fact that everything that happens is subject to divine providence – 'providence' in the descriptive sense discussed earlier – in and of itself offers no guidance as to what you or I ought to do. The events of our lives tell us what is and has been; by themselves they do not indicate what ought to be. For what is and has been includes not only all the goodness and kindness that there has ever been, but all the viciousness and depravity as well.

What is needed to show us what ought to be the case is some ethical standard or standards, some measure of rightness and wrongness. Christians believe that there is such a standard to be found in the *command* of God. It is crucially importance, therefore, when considering the matter of divine providence and divine guidance, to distinguish between the will of God as meaning *what happens*, and the will of God as meaning *what ought to happen*.

These two senses of 'divine will' which we identified earlier when discussing the character of God, are clearly evident in Scripture. Without them it would be impossible to understand the meaning of several crucial passages or to make sense of the whole. For example, Peter stated that Christ had been handed over by God's set purpose and foreknowledge; and that, nevertheless, wicked men had crucified him. What he is in effect saying is that in one sense of 'will' the crucifixion of Christ was against the will of God (for it was a wicked act), while in another sense it was in accordance with his will (for it was an action performed in accordance with the set purpose of God).

Theologians have marked this distinction in various ways. Some have distinguished between the secret will of God (the will that determines what takes place) and the revealed will of God (what God commands), basing this distinction upon Deuteronomy 29:29. The difficulty with this way of highlighting the difference is that not all that God providentially ordains is secret; he sometimes openly reveals what he is about to do. Others have referred to the will of God's good pleasure in contrast to the signified will of God. Still others have referred to the absolute versus the conditional will of God. How the distinction is marked, however, matters less than recognizing the fact that God has two wills. For the distinction is of crucial importance in considering divine providence and guidance, as we shall shortly see.

It is sometimes claimed that there is a serious confusion involved in supposing that God has two wills. For does this not give God a split personality? How can God will what he does not will? It is also maintained that the distinction

131

between the two wills of God is a transparent device to avoid facing a crucial difficulty posed by the occurrence of moral evil on the one hand, and an all-embracing divine providence on the other.

Suppose for the moment that God's providence is 'risky' and there are areas of human action (including human evil action) which God not only does not will, but which he does not know will happen until the events occur. Nevertheless, the events in these areas are *permitted* by God, albeit in a very loose and weak sense. For if God did not allow them, and in some sense support them, then they would not occur. If these events are permitted by God, however, then they are in some sense willed by him even though he is ignorant of what he is willing.

Let us further suppose that at least some of these events permitted by God turn out to be morally evil acts. Then it will follow that God wills (in the sense of permits) the occurrence of certain morally evil actions, actions which are (by definition) contrary to the command of God. God then wills (permits) what he does not will (command), and even perhaps what he cannot will (command). So that the idea of there being two wills of God surfaces again, even on the 'risk' view of providence. So it is not an advantage of that view that it avoids having to think of God having two 'wills'.

Not only is there need, on this 'risk' view of providence, to distinguish between the will of God (decree) from the will of God (command), but a further distinction is necessary. In addition to the two senses of 'will' already distinguished there is a third, namely 'will' in the sense of 'wish'. For on such a view of providence there are many events which God will wish to turn out in a particular way which, due to a person's exercise of free will, will not turn out that way. God's will is capable of frustration; it is reduced to a wish. We shall consider this point further in the later chapter on evil.

The need to distinguish two (or more) wills in God is not simply a consequence of the idea that all events are directly under the providential guidance of God. Rather, any understanding of the relationship between divine activity and human activity which allows that God either wills or permits every action, which recognizes that there are in fact morally evil actions, and which defines some at least of such actions in terms of a breach of a divine command, must employ a distinction between the will of God as command, and the will of God in some other sense.

Nevertheless, it might be claimed that the 'no-risk' view of providence must recognize the two wills in an acute and embarrassing form. For, according to the 'no-risk' view, God controls all events and yet issues moral commands which are disobeyed in some of the very events which he controls. For example, he commands men and women to love their neighbours while at the same time ordaining actions which are malicious or hateful.

This problem is familiar under another guise; it is the problem of evil. It is just *because* it is possible to conceive of two 'wills' in God that the problem of evil arises; the contrast is the familiar one between the omnipotence and the all-goodness of God. As already stated, we shall look at the problem of evil at length in chapter 8.

Granted, then, a distinction (however described) between the precepts or commands of God, and what he in fact brings to pass or allows to be brought to pass, it follows that it is the precepts of God which must prescribe to Christians what they ought, or ought not, to do. What in fact comes to pass, even what comes to pass in the lives of saints, cannot have the force of a prescription. For it is clear from Scripture that God intends his precepts to be guides. What otherwise is their function to be? They prescribe certain courses of action and proscribe others. But what happens or has happened in a person's life, or even in the entire history of the world, could offer no guidance whatsoever to what a person ought or ought not to do. For what has happened includes the whole range of human actions from the saintly to the satanic.

Nor will attempting to anticipate what God will in fact do, and allying oneself with that, offer any better prospect of guidance. For one thing, it is impossible to know in detail what God will do, as we have already noted. Even if we did know, such knowledge could once again offer no moral guidance (about what one ought or ought not to do). But to suppose that we might have such knowledge is probably incoherent. For either the knowledge we would acquire would include the outcomes of our own action or actions between now and the period in the future which we supposedly know about, or it would not. If it does include those outcomes, then we will act in a particular way, and such knowledge could not offer *guidance*. If it does not include those outcomes, then how could the information we receive amount to the knowledge of what will come to pass, since the knowledge, whatever it is, will include gaps to be filled by the outcomes of our own actions?

A person ought to do what God commands, as is repeatedly taught by Jesus (*e.g.*, Mt. 22:34–40) and by the apostles (*e.g.*, Gal. 5:14). Nowhere in Scripture are we taught to look for guidance elsewhere.

The argument that the Christian should be guided, not by what has happened or by what will happen but, by what God prescribes in his law is a very strong one in Scripture. By it a barrier is placed across all those devices, whether they are innocent or malign, that people have devised and advocated for foretelling the future. Tea-leaves, ouija boards, stargazing, necromancy, tarot cards, black magic and all such means for attempting to discover the future (our future, that is) are condemned in Scripture.

This is not because there is not a future to know. We may, with Augustine, claim that the future does not now exist. Nevertheless, the future will exist, it will become present, and what will become present is in the hands of God, known to him. This is clear from the fact of predictive prophecy. What the prophet predicts is not yet happening. Nevertheless it will happen, and the fact that he can predict it shows that at least that segment of the future is known to God, and willed by him. The reason it is wrong to attempt to foretell the future by such means is because they take the Christian away from the appointed way of being guided by God, which is by being obedient to his command.

The claim that Christians ought to be guided by the revealed will of God, stated baldly in this way, does not begin to do justice to the complexities of Christian ethics. There are those situations, for example, which the command of God does not cover, or where duties clash. There are types of action which are neither commanded nor forbidden by God. As both leisure and technological control increase, there seem to be more and more of such decisions. What is the Christian to do? There are decisions to be made which are often complex and personal, where the command of God may offer general guidance but nothing like the detail that is required. Should a Christian move house? Should he or she change job? What is the Christian to do in such circumstances? How can an understanding of the providence of God help?

Part of the agony of such decision-making is that often there does not seem to be any outcome that is obviously the correct and divinely commanded one. Nor, having taken a decision, is there any sign or signal that the correct or incorrect decision has been taken. It is in such circumstances that the temptation to get a definitive view by attempting to peep into the future can be irresistible. While recognizing the complexities – to address them would require a treatise in itself – the argument must stand. Christians ought to resist such a temptation and be guided by the command of God, and their own reasoned application of that command to their circumstances.

It may seem from this discussion as if the doctrine of divine providence plays no part at all in the question of guidance. If the fact that God ordains whatever comes to pass cannot be harnessed in some way to make life more effective and meaningful, then what use is it? Is it not an idle doctrine, one with no practical application?

It would be rash to suppose that the knowledge that God brings everything to pass is of no practical 'operational' benefit. Certainly, as we have emphasized, the order of God's providence cannot be a guide by itself. But a belief in such providence certainly affects the character of a life. For instance, part of the character of the ethical conflict experienced by Christians is formed when they recognize that not every possibility with which they are presented by divine providence represents an opportunity to be grasped. Just because one can do something does not mean one ought to do it.

This can be illustrated from two different kinds of case. Christians may accept God's command (as Abraham did when he offered up Isaac) even though they have every

135

reason to believe that unfavourable consequences (for them or for others) will follow from their obedience to it. God may, in his providence, bring about consequences which those who obey find difficult to accept. Nevertheless, they recognize these consequences not as fate, or as bad luck, but as the hand of God working in ways which at present they find inscrutable.

The fact that the providence of God presents Christians with opportunities does not mean that they ought to seize them, that they represent God's will (in the sense of his command) for them. Here once again we need to distinguish between the descriptive and the normative senses of 'providence'. By the (descriptive) providence of God, King Saul was delivered into David's hands; David had the opportunity to kill him, and was urged to do so. Nevertheless, David refused to recognize this as an opportunity presented by divine providence (normative) which he ought to seize, and refused to touch the Lord's anointed, regarding it as disobedience to God to do so (1 Sa. 24:6; 26:9). We may have the opportunity to steal, to murder or to commit adultery, but this does not mean that we may, much less that we ought, to do any of these things.

The conflict arises from the incompatibility of what God commands with what is happening or is likely to happen. But those who chose to make the opportunities presented by divine providence the rule of their lives would not succeed in avoiding conflict. For these opportunities are multiple; each one represents a choice. It is rare that circumstances are such that there is only one possible outcome, for it is usually possible to do nothing. The fact of choice does not by itself indicate or prescribe which of the alternatives is to be chosen.

But recognition of divine providence, and of the primacy for guidance of the divine command, can also be liberating. Given divine providence, some may be tempted to equate what *is* with what *ought to be*. Let us call such a view *immobilism*. It has seemed to many that because a society has certain practices (say child labour), this is what ought to be, and that any attempt to eliminate the practice is an attempt to flout divine providence. It has been argued on innumerable occasions that the fact that God has permitted or ordained some practice implies that we all ought to accept it as our lot. Apart from the metaphysical difficulties in being a consistent immobilist (for nothing is ever immobile), we can see from our previous discussion that the equation of what *is* with what *ought to be* is unwarranted. Whether what *is* is what *ought to be* depends solely upon whether what *is* corresponds with the revealed will of God, that is, with his command.

It is also tempting to argue the other way, to be a *mobilist*; to argue that the fact that something *is*, means that it ought *not* to be. The fact of a society's social structure being as it *is* represents, the mobilist may argue, a challenge for us to change.

We can see, though, that both the mobilist and the immobilist make the same mistake. They think that we can read off from what *is*, either what *ought to be*, or what *ought not to be*. But of course we cannot. What *is* may or may not coincide with what *ought to be*. The mere fact that it *is* tells us nothing about what *ought to be*, for to know what *ought, or ought not, to be* we must consult not what *is*, but the command of God. It is in such situations that recognition of the distinction between the revealed and the secret will of God can have a liberating effect. We shall look at these matters again in the last chapter.

Providence, tragedy and fate

A more serious difficulty now looms. We have been stressing the place of duty, of obedience to the command of God, in a providential order. Surely, it will be objected, if all things are ordained by God, if all events are under his control, if past, present and future are all alike real to God, what place can there be for significant action of any kind? How can what anyone does influence the outcome of anything? Does not the doctrine of divine providence mean that everything is fated?

This is a common objection to a 'no-risk' view of providence, but I hope it will become clear that it rests upon a mistake. Of course divine providence, of the sort that we have been considering, does place certain restrictions upon what a person can do. But this is merely to say that this doctrine has certain logical consequences. Any doctrine of providence, indeed any doctrine of anything, has logical consequences, ruling out certain matters just as surely as it ensures others.

This doctrine of providence, then, has the consequence that no human decision can change the divine will in any respect. What God has ordained will come to pass. Some may think that such an inability is a disadvantage. It would certainly be so if the divine will were less than perfect, or if it were in some sense incomplete. But such possibilities can safely be ruled out by the Christian. For if God's will were imperfect, then God himself would be so, for he would have a reason for bringing about a situation which was, overall, less than perfect, and this cannot be.

Is the fact that none of us can change the divine will a limitation with which we should be uncomfortable, and which we should attempt to change? It is sometimes said that God cannot sin, or that he cannot tell a lie. Such inabilities might seem to place limitations upon God, limits to his sovereignty. Surely God can do anything, or should be able to do so? But a moment's thought will reveal that this is not so. These inabilities are not like human moral and physical limitations; they are part of what it means to say that God is supremely holy and righteous. Similarly with our supposed inabilities to change the divine will; the fact that we cannot change what is supremely good is hardly a limitation that need bother us.

But does not Scripture frequently say that God's will is changed? Did he not repent that he had created human beings? Did he not, when faced with the unfaithfulness of Israel, almost change his mind about bringing them into the promised land? Again, did he not change his decree about Hezekiah and about Jonah? And did he not, in at least some of these cases, change as a result of human prayer? These facts cannot be denied; nevertheless, when dealing with prayer and providence, I shall defend the view that those theologians have been correct who have argued that such changes are only apparent, not real.

Let us suppose, at least for the moment, that in view of divine providence God's will (what he has decreed) cannot be changed. Is this equivalent to fatalism? It would be fatalistic only if God decreed ends without decreeing any or all of the means to those ends, or if God's will was itself fated.

Some have held that while God has willed certain end points in human history, he has not willed the means to those ends, but has allowed elasticity in the attainment of them. This was the view of the American philosopher William James. He, as we noted earlier, likened God's behaviour to that of a skilful chess player who was able to counter every move made by countless inferior chess players, integrating their games into one unified, consistent whole – the history of the human race.

> The belief in free-will is not in the least incompatible with the belief in Providence, provided you do not restrict the Providence to fulminating nothing but *fatal* decrees. If you allow him (*viz.* God) to provide possibilities as well as actualities to the universe, and to carry on his own thinking in those two categories just as we do ours, chances may be there, uncontrolled even by him, and the course of the universe be really ambiguous; and yet the end of all things may be just what he intended it to be from all eternity.
>
> An analogy will make the meaning of this clear. Suppose two men before a chessboard – the one a novice, the other an expert player of the game. The expert intends to beat ... But he cannot foresee exactly what any one actual move of his adversary may be. He knows, however, all the *possible* moves of the latter; and he knows in advance how to meet each of them by a move of his own which leads in the direction of victory. And the victory infallibly arrives, after no matter how devious a course, in the one predestined form of checkmate to the novice's king.[1]

This is an ingenious analogy. But we have seen that Scripture teaches a *particular* providence, that not only the ends are ordained by God but also the means to those ends. Not a sparrow falls to the ground without his knowledge; he has the hearts of kings in his hands; even arrows drawn at a venture fly to their destined goals.

Is this not fatalistic? Let us *assume* that God has decreed that I shall type a particular letter on my wordprocessor this evening, and that the letter shall consist of certain sentences. (The significance of the fact that this is an *assumption* will emerge in due course.) God, in decreeing that the letter be written, also decrees that I shall write it at a particular time and in a particular way. The natural causal powers that I have are not overridden, or bypassed (as they are in some versions of fatalism), but they are employed through the providence of God in a way that does not impair their voluntariness or spontaneity, my powers of reasoning, or my own personal responsibility in the preparation of the letter. Exactly *how* God does this is not clear, but that he does so has already been established from what the Scriptures teach about the nature and extent of God's providence.

But if I am destined to write the letter, then how can I have any choice in the matter? The answer is that God has ordained that the choice I make to write the letter and rejection of other ways of spending my time on that occasion, together with my choice of the words in the letter, and so on, are some of the very ways in which his will is accomplished. It is crucial, in this regard, that I do not *know* that I am destined to write the letter this evening. (Some argue that I *could not know* this.) For if I did know that I had to write a letter of a particular kind then two things would follow: my usual letter-creating thought processes would be greatly distorted, since I would know that I had to prepare a letter; and the phenomenology of letter-writing (how the business of letter-writing actually presents itself to me) would be drastically different. The beliefs associated with having to prepare such a letter (the details of which I knew God had ordained that I write) would closely approximate to those which I would have if someone were *making* me write such a letter by compelling or constraining me in some way.

This underlines the importance of secondary causes for an understanding of divine providence. The powers of these causes differ greatly. Some are inanimate, such as the powers of chemicals and other physical and organic forces; some are animate, such as the powers of squirrels to climb trees and of snakes to slither; and some are intelligent, notably the powers of adult human beings as they reason and make up their minds. These different powers are real, not phantom. And God, in bringing to pass what he has ordained, typically works *through* these powers not against them or in spite of them.

But let us return for the moment to the letter-writing. It is crucial to the example we are considering that we are *assuming* that God has ordained that I write a particular letter. In fact we do not know this, or anything remotely like it. What we have as we face the future is a matrix of beliefs about the future, as well as wants and reasons and constraints. Among these wants and constraints, for the Christian, is the revealed will of God, what God has commanded. I write the letter, if I am not being compelled to do so by another person, in accordance with my prevailing desires and reasons. The fact that God has ordained that I write a letter is not known in advance, but only in the event, in the outcome.

The importance of causal agency in the production of certain events (which serves to mark off Christianity from fatalism) serves also to mark it off from superstitions of other kinds. Why is it superstitious never to walk under a ladder, or never to have the number thirteen as the number of one's house? It is because there is no known, or even likely, causal connection between walking under ladders, or adopting the number thirteen, and the course of one's life thereafter. If it came to be established that there was such a causal link, then it would be as rational to avoid ladders or the number thirteen as it is rational now to avoid swallowing the contents of jars labelled 'POISON'.

Some argue that the doctrine of divine providence has a flattening or levelling effect upon our understanding of human life. Since every event is ordained by God, then every event must have the same significance as every other event. But why does this follow? Some events are trivial, and some are momentous; some are amusing, whereas some are tragic. We may argue about which are which, as historians perpetually do, but this hardly invalidates the distinction itself. We have seen, also, that for Christians no event can be ultimately tragic, because in the undeserved goodness of God every event in their lives 'works together' for their ultimate

141

good. By the same token the entire life of the unbeliever is a tragedy of disquieting proportions.

Providence and chance

An attempt has been made to show that it does not follow from the fact that God rules and governs all events that there is no place for personal agency. Rather, we have argued, God's providential ordering works through causes. It is in their causal ordering that events are ordained by God, not apart from that ordering.

But what about chance? And, in particular, what about those indeterminacies which, according to modern physics, are at the heart of physical reality? If God upholds that physical reality, as we have also argued, is he not upholding something which is at odds with what we have claimed to be his providential ordering of all events? Perhaps if, after all, events at the most basic physical level are governed by chance, it is only the 'risk' model of divine providence which can do justice to these basic physical facts.

But what is 'chance'? We frequently personify it, and treat chance as if it were an agency. We speak of people arriving by car, and people arriving by chance – but chance is not another, rather ethereal, mode of transportation. It is important to understand that the word 'chance' marks an *absence*, the absence of any imputable cause. So chance is not an agency, like Lady Luck, which takes pleasure in thwarting human schemes and sowing confusion.

But why are some events said to be a matter of chance? One obvious reason is because, due to our ignorance of all the causal factors, it is not possible to predict what happens beforehand. The visitors who arrived by chance did not arrive uncaused, for they arrived at the house by some means. But they did not arrive in accordance with our predictions or expectations, and perhaps they did not arrive in accordance with their expectations either. Similarly, the fact that a machine can deliver numbers randomly, and make the winner of a lottery a matter of chance, does not mean that the generation of the numbers has no cause, but that the pattern of numbers is sufficiently lengthy for us to be unable to predict the next number.

The fact that chance events, in this sense, occur is a reflection upon our own ignorance; but it is important to see that it is no slur on God. Perhaps we should *like* the events which are ordered by God to be more predictable, less random (*i.e.*, less disorderly) than they are. Perhaps we have the idea that, God being who he is, the events *ought to be* more orderly than they are. But there is nothing in the biblical picture of God to support this. God is not capricious, irrational or whimsical in any of his actions. But this does not mean that the reason he does things is obvious. Nor is God bound to follow some pattern of working which is laid down *a priori* by his creatures. God is a God of surprises, and takes pleasure in working in unprecedented ways (from the vantage points of science, and of human religiosity); that is, in ways that are miraculous, or unlikely, or offensive to human presumptions.

There is a stronger sense of 'chance', however; sometimes called 'pure chance'. According to this, what is described as happening by chance has no cause at all; it is absolutely uncaused, and just happens. Heisenberg's Principle is sometimes invoked by theological and other writers as sanctioning such 'pure chance' events at the sub-atomic level, as therefore providing place for human free will, and as making divine providence in a 'non-risk' sense an impossibility. There are those who hold that chance is not wholly a result of our own ignorance, and that such events occur as part of God's overall plan while not expressing his direct intentions. On this view, God is not directly responsible for every single detail of the cosmos. But 'pure chance' is necessary in order that beings arise who are capable of fellowship with God. It follows that on such a view of the universe God takes risks.[2]

But Heisenberg's Principle does not have to be understood as a statement about the absence of causal preconditions in the case of those events which it says are uncertain, but to be about the limits of our knowledge. Even if there are no assignable physical preconditions for a given class of events, it does not follow that these events are *uncaused by God*. For God is not a physical agent on a grand scale, and nothing more. The biblical view is not that God is one physical agent among many (albeit one who is unsurpassably great); it is of a creator who, by his power, upholds the whole of his creation. And it may be, for all we know to the contrary, that God has freely willed into being a succession of events, some of the latter of which are unspecified and unspecifiable in terms of the earlier.

> Belief in a sovereign God does not in the least entail a belief that there *must* be 'hidden physical variables' sufficient to determine the behaviour of electrons on the basis of precedent. For biblical theism all events, equally, with or without precursors according to precedent, need God's say-so in order that they occur at all. The choice of 'God or Chance' is simply not a meaningful alternative, if 'Chance' is meant in the scientific sense. As the Book of Proverbs (ch. 16, v.33) has it: 'The lots may be cast into the lap, but the issue depends wholly on the Lord.'[3]

It would be wrong to suppose that MacKay is arguing here that the mere possibility of such a view makes it credible, as Bartholomew suggests;[4] rather, he is claiming that such a possibility is consistent with biblical theism.

On this understanding of the biblical position, 'chance' is a word for our ignorance. It represents our ignorance of causal factors, perhaps our necessary ignorance. It is not a word for some agent of chaos or meaninglessness, which is set over against God.

6

PRAYER
AND PROVIDENCE

There are many different kinds of prayer commanded and illustrated in Scripture. In this chapter, which brings together prayer and providence, we shall be concerned with only two types, petitionary and intercessory prayers. This is not because other kinds of prayer are not important, but because petitionary and intercessory prayers raise questions about providence. How can God respond to prayer by answering it, when his purposes are changeless? And why, if God is wise and all-knowing, does he need to be prayed to?

The pattern of prayer-and-answer forms part of the narrative of the lives of many prominent Bible characters, for example, Moses, David, Elijah and, in a unique way, Jesus Christ. Yet the practice of petitionary prayer was not intended to cease with the closing of the canon of Scripture. For Christ and the apostles taught that the Christian should pray. Petitionary and intercessory prayer are commanded, just as elsewhere such prayers are forbidden (Je. 7:16). So, asking God and being answered by him is also meant to form part of the life story of any disciple of Christ, as well as of the corporate life of the church.

Petitionary prayers, unlike prayers of thanksgiving and worship, are thus to be thought of as having a certain efficacy upon the actions of the one addressed, a kind of causal efficacy. Certain things happen because people pray, and (it is implied) such things would not happen if people were not to pray. In certain aspects of Christ's teaching, prayer has what might be called a causal threshold. Persistent, importunate prayer is answered in a way that intermittent, half-hearted prayer is not (Lk. 18:7), though elsewhere Christ warns against verbosity and repetition in prayer (Mat. 6:7). The threshold appears to be one of intensity rather than of quantity; efficacy is not in direct proportion to length. Most astonishingly of all, perhaps, on occasion the early disciples were told that their prayers had exceptionless efficacy – *whatever* they asked for would be granted (Mt. 21:22; Jn. 15:16).

Because they have this influence upon God, and because his answers likewise influence human life, both petitionary and intercessory prayers clearly form part of the order of providence, that great matrix of causes and effects through which God governs the world. If prayer may have this efficacy, then it is reasonable to conclude that God is active in certain ways now only because men and women pray or have prayed for certain things to happen or not to happen.

Such a view raises many interesting questions about the divine wisdom and knowledge (for example) – if God knows what will happen, why are prayers necessary (as it seems) to make him do what the petitioner asks? If God is wise, could he not foresee the need to do what he is asked to do without the need for being asked? Or does God change his mind in response to prayer? There are questions about the exact kind of efficacy that prayer may be said to have; about the relationship between God and humankind that such praying presupposes; and about the moral responsibility of the one who prays. We hope to say something about each of these aspects of petitionary and intercessory prayer in this chapter.

As we have seen, providence may be thought of as God's activity now. So prayer and providence are brought together in considering the question, 'How does petitionary or intercessory prayer affect God's activity now?' or 'What part do petitionary and intercessory prayers play in God's activity now?' We noted earlier that one way in which the link between petitionary prayer and providence is made is in connection with personal guidance. For there appear to be many instances in Scripture of God guiding men and women through the answers he gives to their petitionary and intercessory prayers.

Such matters may be thought to pose particular difficulties for the 'no-risk' view of divine providence that we are adopting as our standpoint throughout this book. For it may appear that God is willing to make the fulfilment of his purposes (or even their exact character) depend upon the willingness of men and women to pray, on what they choose to pray for, and on the intensity of their desire in praying. Even aside from these questions, there is the more basic issue of how prayer, and God's response to prayer, can be reconciled with what Scripture has to say about God's unchanging character and purposes (Heb. 6:17 – 18).

We shall tackle some of these questions now, though in rather an oblique way, by looking at what constitutes a personal relationship, and by asking whether the relationship between God and humankind can ever be personal, given a 'no-risk' view of providence.

God, free-will and prayer

One widely made assumption about petitionary prayer is that such prayers can be justified only if both God and human beings possess free wills in the strong sense – the sort that (at least in the case of human beings) seems to be ruled out by a 'no-risk' view of divine providence.

For it is argued that if a relationship between God and human beings is to be truly personal in character, then both parties must be indeterministically free; neither must coerce the other. Only in such circumstances can there be genuine dialogue, and a genuine response to prayer on God's part. If they are genuinely free in this sense, then of course God takes risks, and the 'no-risk' view of providence would have to be abandoned. But it will be argued that the biblical call to petitionary prayer is not nullified by the 'no-risk' view of divine providence that we have been outlining, but is consistent with it, and enhanced by it.

147

According to one widely held assumption about what constitutes a truly personal relationship between God and human beings, it is impossible for God to manipulate creaturely persons and (more importantly in our present context) impossible for those creaturely persons to manipulate God by whatever means, including prayer. Such manipulative prayer would be a form of magic. An example of such thinking is provided by Vincent Brümmer in his book *What Are We Doing When We Pray?* He claims that

> Personal agency is not governed by causal necessity ... but is always the result of the agent's free choice between alternative courses of action. The alternative possibilities are given and might be explained by causal necessity, but the agent's choice is not causally inevitable ... Because they are governed by causal necessity, impersonal objects like machines can be manipulated. I only have to bring about the sufficient causal conditions (*e.g.* by putting a coin in the slot) and the required effects follow with causal inevitability. Persons cannot be manipulated in this way, because someone's decision to act cannot be made causally inevitable. I can try to persuade someone to act by asking him or providing him with good reasons, but his decision to act remains up to him.[1]

On this view, it is only in the context of free, uncoerced personal relations that the idea of a *request* makes any sense. Hence, for a prayer to be a genuine request to God such a context must be presupposed.

> There are three ways in which I could try to get someone else to fulfil my wishes. I could *force* the other to do what I want. In this way I make the other into an object of my causal manipulation and turn the relation between us into a causal one. I could also *command* the other to do what I want. In that case I do not force the other to do my bidding, but I do *oblige* him to do so, and thereby curtail his freedom in responding. I could also *ask* the other to do

what I want. In doing this I renounce the use of constraint toward the other and acknowledge my dependence on the free decision of the other for his response ... This also applies to petitionary prayer: in asking God, the person who prays acknowledges that God is a personal agent, and accepts that he is at the mercy of God's free agency for whatever it is that he asks of God.[2]

It is undeniable that prayer is, or involves, a personal relation between the one who prays and the one who is prayed to. It is doubtful, however, whether the sort of personal relation required in prayer (and indeed personal relations of any kind) requires indeterminism, that is, personal freedom in the strong sense.

A 'personal relation' is difficult to define. Part of the difficulty is that the idea is an abstraction from countless relations between people with differing degrees of power, influence, authority, charisma and so on, over each other. Once this is recognized, and personal relations are not considered in the abstract but in terms of particular examples, then the assumption that coercion or manipulation is logically incompatible with every personal relation becomes questionable. One has to think only of the various ways in which members of a family may influence each other to see that genuine personal relationships need not be, and perhaps cannot be, influence-free and so genuinely free in the way that Brümmer is supposing.

It is clear, however, that personal relations are jeopardized by *some* kinds of manipulation or coercion by one of the parties; for example, by brainwashing or intimidation. But it is surely not a necessary condition of any personal relation that no coercion between the parties can take place. Moreover, a relationship might survive and even thrive upon an appreciable amount of coercion or manipulation if such coercion were benevolently intended.

An example or two may help in supporting this claim. A person A might strongly encourage his friend B to meet C, even making it practically impossible for B to avoid C, because A thinks that although B is reluctant to meet C, he would enjoy or benefit from meeting him. On any realistic appraisal of this situation, A is constraining B. There remains the bare possibility, if indeterminism is presupposed, that B will refuse to be constrained. But in most of such situations this is an unrealistic possibility, whether or not B recognizes that A is constraining him in a certain way. Is this an instance in which the personal relation between A and B breaks down? Hardly.

It might be objected that while the personal relation could survive the constraint described, that constraint is, nonetheless, not an essential part of such a relationship but only an accidental feature of it. It would be hasty to draw such a conclusion, however, for in the case of some such relations coercion is actually constitutive of them. Thus constraint may be part of the relationship between a parent and a child, a husband and a wife, a teacher and a student, or a manufacturer and a customer, in such a way that the relationship would not be intelligible without it. It is hard to imagine that this fact makes all such relationships sub-personal in character.

At the heart of such claims, when they are applied to the matter of petitionary prayer, appears to be the assumption that prayer is a personal relationship between equals, founded upon a mutual contract between them. This is hardly the biblical picture of God's relationship to human-kind, and in any case there are numerous personal relations which are not founded upon mutual contract. For example, the unchosen obligations that arise in the family, the church and the state are non-contractual. Thus membership of a family is not a symmetrical relation. Father and son are not equals. Nor, except in very unusual circumstances, does membership of a family depend upon a decision. A parent is in a position of authority, and has certain moral and legal responsibilities for the child, and not vice versa. Does this make it less than a full personal relation, or only a *qualified* relation? The difficulty with supposing that this is so is that many more personal relations have such asymmetries. For each of us has particular combinations of roles and responsibilities not exactly replicated by others whom we meet and with whom we have personal relations, or at least so we believe. Indeed, one is struck by the fact that a situation in which personal relations are exactly symmetrical constitutes a rare, limiting case of such relations, and is often artificial and abstract. As Harry Frankfurt puts it, 'There must be limits to our freedom if we are to have sufficient personal reality to exercise genuine autonomy at all. What has no boundaries has no shape.'[3]

If, as it is plausible to assume, any such asymmetries provide occasions for the exercise of constraints like that exercised by A on a friend B, then there are very few kinds of personal relations in which such constraints are absent. And perhaps, from the point of view of constructing a philosophical account of personal relations, they are only of minor importance. The inherited obligations that we have mentioned may be regarded as a divine gift, the providential gift to each of us of a self. It is from this self, in its concrete relationships with other selves, that our volitions and desires engage with those of others. Any account of personal relations which denied or ignored this would be deficient.

It is implied by what Brümmer and others have said that if a 'no-risk' view of providence is accepted, then, as far as divine-human relations are concerned, God could not have a truly personal relation with any person. Instead, he would be reduced to manipulating that person, and in turn that person would be reduced to attempting to manipulate God by means of petitionary prayer. But we can now see that this is a mistake. The alternatives are not (a) non-manipulation only if a relation is truly personal, or (b) manipulation. For we have seen that there are elements of constraint in a wide range of human relationships, and that a relationship without any constraint is hardly recognizable as being human.

It is also a mistake to suppose that every instance of making a request, for example, excludes any degree of pressure whatever. A person can ask with differing degrees of emphasis and pressure. ('I ask you for the last time; did you borrow my copy of *The Phenomenology of Spirit*?') Think of the varieties of *asking* that there are.

For this reason, personal relations are consistent with an appreciable element of predictability. In fact, it can plausibly be argued that the closer the relationship between people,

151

(the relation of friend to friend, say), the more predictable the responses of each to the other may become. This is part of what is meant by 'a stable relationship'. Predictability is necessary for the stability, and stability is generally regarded as a desirable, if not an essential, feature of human relationships.

It could be argued, then, that whether or not providence is 'no-risk' is at the very least irrelevant to the reality of personal relations. But, it might be objected, if one party in a relationship knowingly exercises an influence upon the other so as to rule out any risk, does such an influence not destroy the relationship?

It all depends upon how such influence is exercised. If it is exercised through the personality of the one involved, through the matrix of his desires and beliefs, then it is hard to see that that factor alone makes for less than a fully personal relationship. It is very difficult to be dogmatic on this question because of the great variety of factors that can be regarded as coercive. If A points out to B that B's intended course of action has fearful consequences, is A attempting to coerce B? And if pointing out these consequences results in B not carrying out that intention, has B been coerced? It is not clear what answer ought to be given to these questions. If the absence of risk is due to physical coercion, however, then its destructiveness of personal relations is much clearer.

Tentatively, therefore, I propose the following two conditions as at least sufficient for a personal relation. A relation between two human beings, or between a human being and God, is personal when (a) that relationship is exercised through the structure of belief and desire of each, and (b) that exercise does not rely upon physical coercion or psychological compulsion. This second condition is included even though the boundaries between such coercion and compulsion (on the one hand) and acceptable interpersonal constraint (on the other) are unclear and controversial.

If these conditions are reasonable, then the question whether the resulting relationship is partly predictable by one or other of the parties (and hence is a 'no-risk' relationship) is irrelevant. And the question of whether it is predictable in principle is then irrelevant. So, in turn, the question of whether providence is risky or risk free is irrelevant to an understanding of personal relations.

The efficacy of petitionary prayer

If there is no objection in principle to prayer in a 'no-risk' providential order being a case of an interpersonal relation, then how are we to understand the efficacy of prayer, the way in which it contributes to the unfolding of God's providential purposes?

This is a crucial question. For whatever the strengths and weaknesses of the 'no-risk' view of providence, nothing can be allowed to detract from the teaching of Scripture and the conviction of Christians that God brings about certain events because people ask him to (Jas. 1:5). So graphic is Scripture's teaching on this that God is often represented as one who not only makes up his mind in response to prayer, but who also changes his mind because of prayer (Is. 38:1–6). But is a 'no-risk' view of providence inconsistent with this biblical teaching?

The efficacy of petitionary prayer is no more or less problematical than that of any other action which a person may perform in a 'no-risk' providential order. The problem arises in the first place only because 'prayer' is thought of in too abstract a fashion, as if it were a cosmic force or principle. In what follows we shall, as far as possible, treat prayer like any other human action, though we shall assume that praying is subject to a structure of commands and prohibitions. In other words, we shall assume that there is a *morality* of praying, just as there is a morality of performing other actions. Prayer is warranted because God commands it under certain conditions and circumstances, permits it in some circumstances, and forbids it in others.

As we have seen, in Scripture prayer is commanded by God, while at other times it is allowed by him, or forbidden by him. Thus, to have any prospect of being answered, a petitionary prayer must be warranted by God, at least by being permitted. Prayer to God, at any time, under any condition, about anything, is not a natural human right. What exactly

153

the circumstances are in which prayer to God is warranted by him would be a matter for consideration in a more detailed and thorough treatment of prayer than we are able to carry out in the present study.

Nevertheless, it should be stressed that whether a particular prayer or type of prayer is warranted can be answered only by a careful induction of the biblical data. The results of that induction are vital. If they show that there are certain prayers which, if asked sincerely, will always be answered, or answered only sometimes, or never answered, then this is obviously relevant to dealing with such questions as 'Did God answer because I prayed, or for some other reason?'

The position that we start from, given our other assumptions – particularly the 'no-risk' view of divine providence – is that if anyone prays, then God has ordained the prayer. The praying is thus an action in the order of divine providence like any other action. If we were to assume a 'risky' view of providence, then another account of the efficacy of petitionary prayer would need to be sought. Readers may care to work out for themselves what that account would be.

Why is it important to bear in mind that God has ordained the activity of praying under certain circumstances? It is important if we are to resist the temptation to separate the action of praying from the matrix of other actions and events in which it is set, and to speculate about 'the power of prayer' in isolation. It is easy to ask, 'if A had not prayed, would God have done what he did?' But to do so is in effect to prise apart the action of praying from the total matrix of events and actions of which it forms a part.

Suppose that a person works hard at some examinations, prays for success in them, and passes. It is very tempting to suppose that the petitionary prayer could not have had any efficacy, and that the person's hard work was itself causally sufficient for the examination success. It is clearly unsatisfactory as an account of petitionary prayer to limit the efficacy of the praying to the petitioner, as if the sole effect of the prayer to God were to make the petitioner redouble his or her efforts and so succeed. Perhaps the examinee's prayer did have this effect; but if this is all that such a prayer ever accomplished then prayer would be nothing more than talking to oneself.

Why are such attempts at prising apart one or other action, whether it is praying or some other action, from the matrix of events and actions to be resisted? We should resist them because, if it is supposed that A had not prayed, then the total matrix of events and actions is thereby changed. A different matrix is introduced since the original situation *did* involve praying. Whether the question 'If A had not prayed, what would have happened?' is worth discussing very largely depends upon how much *general* information there is about such cases, and therefore in how warranted we are in making generalizations about them. For instance, we have sufficient general information about the germination of seeds to accept the truth of the statement, 'If the seeds had not been watered they would not have germinated.' But do we have sufficient information to determine the truth or otherwise of the statement, 'If A had not prayed for examination success, he or she would have failed?' Assuming that A's prayer was warranted, do we know enough either about A or about God's intentions, to draw that conclusion?

One important difference between praying to God and watering the seeds is that prayer is a *request*. How otherwise similar the cases are depends upon how much is known about the request. Suppose, for example, that it is known that God will invariably grant such a request. Then the 'because' in 'God helped Smith because he prayed' and in 'The seeds germinated because they were watered' are of similar force. The 'because' signals, in each case, that, given certain conditions – a uniform determination to grant a prayer on the one hand and certain uniformities about plant growth on the other – the human action is *sufficient* to bring about the result.

Are there any circumstances in which a petitionary prayer would be a sufficient condition for God to act, the very fact of praying ensuring that what is prayed for is granted? Are there circumstances such that if these circumstances occurred, and Jones asked God for something in those circumstances, the request would invariably be granted?

In order to approach this question, let us imagine the following non-theological case. A promises B that should B at any time want to borrow A's ladders, then all B needs to do is to ask for them. This certainly looks like a case of a personal relation. A and B, let us suppose, are friends; and A's promise looks like a personal, friendly, intentional action. What the promise appears to do is to specify a sufficient condition for a request being granted. To obtain the ladders, all that B needs to do is ask, and the ladders will be his.

Is there any reason to think that what is true of this non-theological example cannot be true of a parallel theological case? Suppose that God were to say, quite generally, to anyone who hears, 'If you seek me you shall find me' (understanding this as a promise and not as a mere prediction). If Jones seeks God, then, assuming that God's promise holds good, Jones will find God; his seeking, given the promise, is a sufficient condition of his finding God.

Not only is this possible, but, given what Scripture says about the place of divine promises in prayer, as well as what we know about the history of Christian piety, it is a sort of case that is central to an understanding of petitionary prayer. If this example is coherent, then it cannot be true that whatever is causally sufficient is manipulative. Nevertheless, the causal sufficiency that it exhibits is not mechanistic. The prayer's efficacy comes through the pre-establishment of *warrants*, such as promises or threats, which may in turn be informal and tacit, or formalized through issued regulations and codes of practice. And whether or not the causally sufficient condition is fulfilled can be ascertained only through understanding what is said. But with these provisos, the types of cases cited form a family of cases where causal sufficiency is an integral part of a personal relation and at the same time is not a case of manipulation.

There are instances where God has promised in a uniform or exceptionless way to answer certain prayers, and instances where he has not, but where he has reserved to himself the right to answer or not as he sees fit. In addition, there may be situations where *only* prayer is efficacious, where God indicates that certain events will take place *only if* people pray.

One upshot of this discussion is that it is important not to split apart, without sufficient justification, the making of promises from other actions within which the warrant to make petitionary prayers is set. If we do venture to make the split, then there will be different results according to the different circumstances in which the prayer is set.

At one extreme, it is safe to infer that, if the prayer had not been offered, what happened would not have happened. At the other extreme, it may be equally safe to infer that, had the prayer not been offered, the event prayed for would have occurred anyway. But in between these two extreme situations there is a large middle ground in which the cases are not clear one way or the other, and speculation is unsafe.

One consequence of this is that any investigation into the efficacy of petitionary prayer ought not to be conducted as if it were a scientific investigation. The natural sciences are *sciences* in virtue of the repeatability of experimental situations and the possibility of establishing, by such means, generalizations of timeless regularity. Prayer, however, is not one physical factor – like a chemical or a mechanical force – among many other such forces in a set of physical equations. Prayer is set among divine and human actions and their significance in the one, unrepeatable history of the universe. In this history, the particular matrix of divine and human actions that we choose to isolate for discussion is unique and unrepeatable. It is not, like some aspects of the unfolding history, replicable by scientists virtually at will. Hence, to ask what would have been the case if that unique matrix had been different with respect to a non-repeatable situation is to ask a question that is unanswerable.

This can be expressed in more theological fashion as follows. God, who ordained certain ends, also ordained the means to accomplish those ends. Now in some cases, in God's wisdom, the means include people warrantably asking him to do certain things. He has so ordered the total matrix that he does some things because people ask him to, and, if they had not asked, the conditions which are otherwise sufficient – apart, that is, from the request – for the production of what is asked for would not have been provided. In the words of the hymn-writer Joseph Hart:

> Prayer was appointed to convey
> The blessings God designs to give.

157

Or, in the words of Augustine, 'So, too, prayers are useful in obtaining those favours which He foresaw He would bestow on those who should pray for them.'[4]

This discussion of petitionary prayer also largely applies to intercessory prayer, where God is asked to provide for the needs of others. Among petitionary prayers, however, are prayers for those matters which Christians believe, on the authority of God, will happen unconditionally. For instance, Christians are invited to pray for the coming of God's kingdom, knowing that God's kingdom will inevitably come. How are we to understand such prayers?

A little earlier it was argued that there may be cases in which God has unconditionally promised that whoever asks for something receives it. But praying 'Your kingdom come' is a rather different case from this. It is a case not of God unconditionally promising X if X is prayed for, but of God unconditionally promising X whether or not X is prayed for. For as far as one can judge from Scripture, the coming of the kingdom of God is unconditional. This naturally leads to the question, 'If the coming of the kingdom is promised whether or not it is prayed for, what is the sense in praying for it?' The answer must be that, despite their grammatical appearance, such prayers are not petitions so much as expressions of desire, an affirmation of solidarity with the unfolding will of God.

A moral problem about prayer

Let us consider again the idea of petitionary and intercessory prayer based upon a 'risky' view of providence, in which a causally indeterminate view of human and divine action is assumed. If one of the aims of maintaining such a view is to make petitionary and intercessory prayer truly efficacious by setting it in an interpersonal context in which participants have indeterministic free wills, then the consequences for human personal responsibility are alarming. For if this view is taken seriously, it appears to place much if not the whole of the burden of responsibility for the success or failure of the prayer for the occurrence or non-occurrence of the divine action prayed for upon the one who intercedes (or who fails to intercede).

For if some particular evil will be averted if, and only if, an intercessor properly intercedes for its removal, then the burden of responsibility for the continuing evil falls squarely upon the shoulders of the intercessor. The evil continues, on this view, only because the intercessor has not prayed sufficiently fervently, or sincerely, or at sufficient length, for its removal. It then becomes valid to argue not only 'if only A had prayed harder, X would have been averted'; but also, 'only if A had prayed harder (more faithfully, *etc.*) would X have been averted.'

Who is to blame for Auschwitz? If petitionary and intercessory prayer is commanded by God, then failure to pray is disobedience. But the culpability involved in failing to pray in a 'risky' providential order is much greater. For, on this view of petitionary prayer, the blame at least for the continuation of the atrocity (once it has come to the notice of a potential intercessor) falls not on Nazi Germany, or on God, but on the numerous potential intercessors who did not pray as hard or as sincerely as they might have done. Whether or not such a view is in accordance with Scripture and mainstream Christian belief is open to question. Another similarly serious objection is that the burden of such failure upon any petitioner would be insupportable.

Whatever its defects may be, petitionary prayer based upon a 'no-risk' view of divine providence does not have this problem. On this view, prayer is a God-ordained means of fulfilling what God wills. Intercessory prayer is not one means of settling God's mind on a course of action, but one of the ways in which the already settled mind of God effects what he has decreed. So the 'burden of responsibility' for the answering or not answering of intercessory prayers (if one is permitted to use that expression) is placed firmly upon shoulders wide and strong enough to bear it, the shoulders of God himself.

On the 'no-risk' view of intercessory prayer the mind of God is not a *tabula rasa*, waiting to be imprinted with the requests of the intercessors. It is already imprinted with his own will. The relation between an intercession and its answer or refusal is thus non-natural or conventional in character; it is related to the character of God's pre-established will.

To illustrate this, let us suppose the existence of a rich, powerful and benevolent agency. Two identical requests, say for a sum of money, are made to it. One is granted and the other is refused. The only explanation for this which is open to someone who takes the 'risk' view of intercession must be one which cites some natural obstacle in the one case that is not present in the other, a hidden causal factor in the situation.

On the 'no-risk' view, the explanation lies in the will of the agency, and thus not in terms of natural forces, such as the loudness and force of the request, or any other of its features. Perhaps the difference is to be explained by the fact that, for example, the agency had an agreement with one of the people making the request to make payment upon request, but had no such agreement with the other. Perhaps there was an obligation on the agency to make payment to the one and not to the other.

To conclude, why is *any* prayer answered? The answer to that question cannot be in terms of the benevolence of God, since that proves too much. If the reason one prayer is answered is that God is benevolent, then why are not all prayers answered? Nor can the answer be in terms of the strength of the intercessor, on whom would be placed an insupportable burden for those intercessions which fail through weakness, or which are never made. The answer must be, therefore, not natural but conventional in character. The explanation why some prayers are answered and some are not must lie in terms of the structure of will and warrant established by God himself.

160

7

PROVIDENCE AND ACCOUNTABILITY

In chapter 2 the contrast between 'risk' and 'no-risk' views of providence was drawn. It was argued that it is possible to do justice to the biblical data, and to the classical Christian idea of providence as the purposive guidance of God extending over all events, only by understanding providence as involving no risks for God. In that chapter we also examined the ambitious claim that, through postulating 'middle knowledge' for God, it is possible both to maintain a strong, libertarian sense of human freedom and a 'no-risk' view of providence. It was argued there that this view founders upon the obscurity and possible incoherence of the very idea of a middle knowledge of what creatures will freely do, when freedom is understood in an indeterministic sense.

There may be other ways of maintaining human freedom, in this strong sense, in a way that is consistent with the 'no-risk' view of providence. The remainder of this study, however, will be conducted on the assumption that it is likely that only an account of human freedom which is compatible with some form of determinism is in accord with the 'no-risk' view of divine providence. To readers who disagree with this an earlier invitation is reissued: to make their own adjustments to the ensuing discussion which their own preference for a 'risk' view of providence, or for a 'no-risk' view involving middle knowledge, requires.

In this chapter and the next we shall attempt to develop some of the implications of the 'no-risk' view. But there is no escaping the difficulty of the issues involved. For reasons of space, and so as not to overbalance the book as a whole, it will not be possible to provide anything like an exhaustive treatment of all the issues. It is hoped, nevertheless, to offer the main lines of argument and to indicate those places where further work needs doing, and to cite some of the relevant literature in what has become a vast field of enquiry.

Readers, who for any of several reasons may feel unable to take a 'no-risk' view of divine providence, or who favour middle knowledge, may also wonder what purpose would be served by reading on. It is hoped that in considering what follows they will at least be able to clarify their own ideas further, even if they find what is written totally unpersuasive.

The problems

The problems that confront us are of two main kinds. The first concerns the best way of thinking about the relation between divine and human activity in a world of free[1] and responsible creatures upheld and directed by God. This is the *metaphysical* issue of God's relation to the world. It is in effect a problem – the chief problem – that arises in what we have called the first context of interest in divine providence. God's relation to the world not only raises the question of preserving the distinctness of God from his creation, but also of preserving the distinction between divine responsibility and human responsibility. The basic question, then, has to do with the very nature of the division and connection between divine and human reality.

In addition, there is a moral problem of a direct kind – in fact, two moral problems. Granted that God is distinct from his creation, and that there are matters for which God is responsible and for which his creatures are not, and vice versa, there is the question of how God can (morally

speaking) permit evil in a world which he has created, sustains and directs. How is it consistent with the overall character of God, and in particular with his goodness, that there
should be evil of the kind and to the degree that there is?

This question is particularly acute for the 'no-risk' view.
For if men and women are free in a sense that is compatible
with determinism, then God could have created human
beings and ensured that they never sinned. (If people are
indeterministically free, it has been plausibly argued that not
even God could have created a person such that that person
did only what was morally right.)[2]

The question how God can permit evil in such a universe is
perhaps the chief question that arises in the second context.
For the Christian message of salvation, and the existence of
the church as the bearer of that message, make sense only if
there is evil for which men and women are culpable. But it is
also a problem in the third context – how ought a person to
think of and respond to evil in his own life? We shall look at
the problem of evil in connection with the 'no-risk' view of
providence in the next chapter.

The second moral question has to do with human action.
The problem of moral evil naturally presupposes that there
are morally evil actions – not only actions with evil consequences, but actions for which an individual person is to be
held responsible. And the main question in this area is: is the
freedom which (I have argued earlier) is alone compatible
with 'no-risk' providence that kind of freedom which is also
sufficient for human responsibility of this sort? This chapter
is devoted to developing an answer to this question.

God's relation to the universe

The relationship between the divine creator and his creation
is *sui generis*. There is no other relation which exactly parallels
one which is both so close and yet so distinct, and which is so
all-encompassing, deriving from the fact that the creator
upholds all aspects and details of his creation by his power at
each moment of their existence, and directs these details to
an appointed end, and yet is not himself a part of the
creation.

Two extreme reactions loom into view at this point, each of which has its attractions. On the one hand, because of the difficulty of these issues, it is tempting to say no more about them; or to have recourse to paradox. For we are dealing with matters not only of which human beings have no experience, but of which they *could* have no experience. On the other hand, it is also tempting to try to offer a *theory*: something that will, like a scientific theory, offer an explanation of this unique relationship and so make it intelligible.

Each of these approaches is, in my view, to be resisted. For unless one is going to grant that there is a fundamental incoherence at the heart of God's relationship to the world – which is in effect to say that there is no relationship at all, for there are no relationships which are incoherent – then there is *some* consistent account of that relationship. There is a true account, if only we could comprehend it. And unless it is argued that there is a blanket prohibition on attempts to think coherently and consecutively about this relationship. then it would appear to be at least permitted to do so; it may even be the duty of some to do so.

Nevertheless, because of the unique character of God's relation to the world, a great deal of caution needs to be exercised. For the exact nature of that relationship may be beyond our comprehension. Indeed, given that the character of God is beyond our full comprehension, it is highly likely that his relationships to the various features of his creation will be so as well. So how are we to proceed?

I suggest we ought to proceed by considering *models* of the relationship between God and his responsible creatures which Scripture sets forth. What would such a model be like? It would be a worked-out way of thinking about one or other aspect of the divine-human relationship. It would do at least two things: it would provide a coherent way of thinking about that relationship which does justice to at least some of the main scriptural data on the matter, and would not go beyond those data by knowingly violating other scriptural data.

So any such model then must be constrained by the biblical data. For instance, it must preserve God's providential control over all particularities; it must avoid representing human agents as being compelled to act (so compromising their freedom and responsibility); and it must avoid making God the author of sin in such a way as to imply that he is less than wholly good.

But the Bible says very little, if anything, to illuminate the unique relationship between God and his creation. That relationship undergirds everything else, and is *assumed*. Further, as we saw earlier, Scripture refers both the occurrence of evil, and the apparent injustice and inequity of life, to the lordship of God. Job did this; and when Paul considered the objection that it was unfair of God to find fault with those who cannot resist his will, he retorted: 'Shall what is formed say to him who formed it, "Why did you make me like this?"' (Rom. 9:20).

These scriptural data strongly suggest that one appropriate and sufficient way of responding to the problem of evil, and to the question of the divine responsibility for evil, is to assert divine sovereignty in an unqualified way. Anyone who wished to end the discussion of these issues at that point would be on solid biblical ground: 'Will not the Judge of all the earth do right?' (Gn. 18:25).

Why then attempt to go further? Is there not danger in going beyond the explicit teaching of Scripture? Such danger must be weighed against the advantage to be gained by blocking off false inferences that may be drawn from such data.

An example from another area of theology may make this clear. Scripture claims that the Word of God became flesh (Jn. 1:14). As it stands this is an admirable statement of the incarnation; it cannot be bettered. But it is open to misunderstanding. In becoming flesh, did the Word cease to be the Word? Does 'the flesh' refer to a human body, to human nature, or to sinful human nature? A worked-out christology is designed to meet such questions, not by explaining the dogma away but by guarding it from misunderstanding. One way of thinking about the various models of divine and human action which we shall now review is as possible means of protecting statements such as those of Job and Paul, and parallel statements about human accountability, from false inferences.

Some have argued, however, that the whole project of constructing an account of divine providence in which God is

165

shown not to be the author of sin is unnecessary – not because the idea of God's being the author of sin is an acceptable one, but because in virtue of who God is the question of whether or not he is the author of sin cannot arise. Or, more precisely, in view of who God is, the inference that if he is the author of sin then he is himself morally evil or tainted, cannot arise.

Thus Brian Davies has argued that God is not a moral agent, and that it is only moral agents who can have their actions morally assessed.

> It is commonly said that a moral agent is someone able to do his duty, someone capable of living up to his obligations. But it seems very hard to see how the God of classical theism can be thought of as having duties or obligations. These normally confront people in social contexts, in contexts where there are other people around. But, according to classical theism, God is the source of all beings.[3]

For God is not just an extraordinary person; he is the source of all beings, and not himself a being. Furthermore, an individual is a moral agent only if that person has duties and obligations. But God has no duties; he does not dwell in a social context which is required for such duties to be intelligible. Nor does it make sense to talk of God either succeeding or failing in an enterprise. Hence his performance cannot be assessed – even by himself.

Here is a debate that is characteristic of philosophy but one which is extraordinary under any other circumstances. On the one hand, there are those (such as Aquinas and Anselm) who argue that in virtue of the moral goodness and impeccability of God he cannot be regarded as the author of sin. For, to be the author of sin, he would have to be evil. On the other hand, there are those (such as Brian Davies) who argue that it is in virtue of God's unique role as the creator and source of all being that the question of his moral assessment cannot arise. It almost seems as if the very reason that leads one party to avoid imputing sinfulness to God is the reason which leads others to say that sinfulness cannot be imputed to him.

Almost, but not quite. For Davies is not arguing that God is not good, that he is an amoral God for whom any action, however evil, is consistent with his character. Nor is he arguing, as some have done, that God's power is such that whatever he commands or permits, morally speaking, is morally right. Rather, Davies is maintaining the goodness of God but arguing that in virtue of being changeless and incapable of failure, and being the creator of all beings, God is incapable of acting in a way which permits moral assessment. And if he cannot be assessed morally, then we cannot say of him that what he did or permitted was evil; or, for that matter, that it was good.

This may seem to be a neat sidestepping of the problem, but it is open to at least two objections. The first is that according to the Christian faith God is good. Davies would not deny this. But he would deny that God is morally good. But what sort of goodness might God have that is not *moral* goodness? What is the concept of non-moral goodness? We speak sometimes of good knives and good motorcars, but here we are using 'good' in a purely functional or instrumental sense; good *as a knife*. But such a sense is hardly relevant here; we can make little sense of the idea that God is good as God.

It is hard, therefore, to grasp the idea of a goodness which is neither a moral nor a functional goodness, but which God has supremely and which renders him worshipful. And this brings us to the second objection. If God is worshipful as good (because of his goodness), then that goodness must bear some fairly close relationship to the goodness which, from time to time, we ascribe to human actions and which is ascribed supremely to Christ. Scripture warns us against creating a God in our own image, consequently we must always allow for the real possibility that our ideas about God are mistaken and in need of revision. Nevertheless, even allowing for this, the goodness of God must bear some positive relation to the sorts of human actions we regard as good. Otherwise, why ascribe *goodness* to God?

For these reasons I do not think that Davies' proposal to sidestep the issue of the implication of God in human moral evil succeeds.

There is, then, no alternative to considering various

167

systematic ways of thinking about God's relationship to his creation by the use of 'models'. In what follows, two or three such models will be examined in an effort not only to throw light on the unique relationship between God and his creation, but also to preserve the scriptural data against false models and unwarranted inferences. Each of the models to be considered has exerted considerable influence in the history of Christian thought about divine providence.

Model 1: evil as a privation

Scripture teaches that, as far as the original creation is concerned, all was created good. That included human beings; their actions were good. That is, not only did their actions conform to the standard of rightness and wrongness which God ordained for the flourishing of the human race, but all such actions proceeded from good motives. They were motivated by love to God and love to neighbour. Thus the goodness of the original creation was, in part at least, a moral goodness.

Moral evil, particularly the evil of a bad motive or intention, is thus a deformation. This has been one of the reasons why theologians have represented evil actions as the corruption and depravity of the good. The pain and suffering arising from such deformed human relationships are real; nevertheless, they proceed from what is negative, from deformation or depravity. Evil is thus corruption, decay, deficiency, perishing. This is why, in Scripture, sin is represented as a lack; as a coming short of the divine glory (Rom. 3:23), and as a departing from God (Heb. 3:12).

To say that evil is a lack is not to say that it is non-existent, for then it would be literally *nothing*. Rather, the evil consequences of evil arise from what is essentially a defect, just as the stumbling and lack of mobility which may follow from blindness are real enough as effects, but they follow from a condition which is the *absence* of sightedness.

One might thus analyse many human actions as having a moral and a non-moral component. Showing an old lady across the road may be an intentional action with psychological and physical aspects to it. But the inner-directedness of the action, the intention or motive which gives rise to it or at least colours it, is not physical and not merely psychological. It is the directedness of the action which determines its goodness or badness, according to whether it has been done out of love for neighbour and for God, or for some other reason.

According to this model, in so far as such an action is considered as a psychological and physical activity, it can be regarded as being causally upheld by God in accordance with his sustaining agency as creator. The same applies if the action is morally good, since all goodness proceeds from God. But in so far as the action is morally evil, it is deficient in the ways described. Not only does God not cause the evil directedness of the action, but because he is all-good he *could not* cause the action to have such a direction.

Such a model has been a recurrent theme of Christian reflection on providence and human action. For example, Augustine writes:

> For what is that which we call evil but the absence of good? ... What are called vices in the soul are nothing but privation of natural good.[4]

And Anselm:

> When a person uses a sword, for instance, or uses language, or the power of speaking, it is the same sword or language or power whether he uses it correctly or incorrectly. The same is true of the will. As with reason, which we use for reasoning, so the will is not one thing when we use it correctly and something different when we use it incorrectly. A substance or an action is said to be just or unjust according to the will. But what the will essentially is, is neither more nor less when it is just than when it is unjust. Thus, God causes both the essential being and the goodness of all good wills and good works. And He causes the essential being of all evil wills and evil works, but He does not cause their being evil. For even as a thing's being is from God alone, so its rightness is from Him alone.[5]

169

And Aquinas:

> But sin can be called a being and an action only in
> the sense that something is missing. And this miss-
> ing element comes from a created cause, i.e. the free
> will in its departure from order to the First Agent
> who is God.
>
> Accordingly, this defect is not ascribed to God as
> its cause, but to the free will, just as the limp in a
> cripple comes from his deformity and not from his
> power to move even though this power enables him
> to limp.[6]

So God upholds the agent in his action, and the action itself,
and permits but does not bring about the evil intent, because
he cannot, being good, do so.

This might be explained further as follows. A person's
action can be described at various levels. One and the same
action can be described as moving one's arms and feet;
driving a car; driving a car in Liverpool; driving to one's bank
in Liverpool; driving to rob one's bank in Liverpool. And the
view we are outlining could be expressed by stating that God
upholds all aspects of such an action, except that aspect which
warrants us in truly describing the action as a morally bad
action.

We may ask, however, 'What or who causes an evil action?
What are its causes?' The following answer suggests itself.
What determines it are the normal causes of action, human
intentions and the like, which God ordains and upholds as he
ordains and upholds everything. But what determines the
action in so far as it is an *evil* action is a divine *withholding*. God
withholds his goodness or grace, and forthwith the agent
forms a morally deficient motive or reason and acts accordingly. So while God ordains and sustains and foreknows the
evil action he does not positively will it, as he positively wills
good and gracious actions. Here is an important asymmetry
in God's relation to what is morally good and morally evil.

Because sin or moral evil is a privation, the only cause or
author of a morally evil act is whoever is the immediate
author of it. God cannot, for reasons already given, be the

immediate cause of evil, even though he ordains it, and so knows what particular evil action, in given circumstances, a moral agent will perform.

This view has the undoubted advantage that it preserves God from being the author of sin consistently with the 'no-risk' view of providence. The price to be paid for that is the adoption of the privative or deficient view of sin. But perhaps with sufficient safeguards and careful explanation this is not such a great price to pay.

Model 2: divine permission

The strength of the idea of evil as a lack or privation is that it provides a reason in the very nature of things why God cannot be the author of sin; he cannot, because God is the all-good creator. What God creates is good: how could the one in whom all fulness of being resides create a moral lack or deficiency? Yet the idea of evil as a privation is obscure: how can a lack, something which is *not*, bring about horrendous evils in the world?

So privation has its difficulties. Nevertheless, it provides a key idea which is central to a second model for understanding divine providence and human agency – the idea of the divine *permission* of evil. Even if privation makes no sense, it still follows from God's impeccable character that he could not perform an evil action; he could not (in the phrase that has become common) 'be the author of sin'. So how do evil actions happen, if God's providence is in control of everything, and nevertheless he cannot bring about evil? The answer is by his permission. God allows evil.

It is possible to think of permission in two ways, or as having two strengths: general or specific. For example, John may be leaving the country and gives his friend Joe permission to use his car while he is away. This is general permission; no particular uses of the car are specified. While Joe has the car he may go in it wherever he wants. Although John, by his permission, is *affecting* Joe's movements (for Joe now has the use of a car), he is not *controlling* his movements.

The idea of general permission has been favoured by those who hold one version or another of the 'risk' view of divine providence. But it is hard to see how general permission of this kind could be compatible with the control which, according to the 'no-risk' view, God exercises over his creation. If God granted general permission for people to do evil, this is equivalent to granting them the power to do action A or B or C and so on *ad infinitum*. Then whichever evil action was performed would be wholly up to them, and God would have to await the outcome. This is clearly incompatible with the 'no-risk' view.

So, on the 'no-risk' view, the permission in question must be *specific* We might suppose the situation to be as follows: God ordains all those circumstances which are necessary for the performance by a person of a particular morally evil action (say, an action of cruelty at a particular time and place). God does not himself perform that action, nor could he, for the reasons already given. Nevertheless, he *permits* that action to take place. He does not prevent it to stop it. So in the circumstances ordained by God someone does an evil action; the circumstances are ordained, but the evil is permitted.

The force of appealing to divine permission is considerable when it is remembered that God, being all-powerful, *could* have prevented the action in question being performed. He could do so, most drastically, by annihilating the person, or less drastically, by diverting or distracting the person from carrying out the action. And perhaps, for all we know, God in fact prevents many evil actions in this way. Perhaps, thanks to God's preventings, there is much less evil in the world than there would otherwise be.

> If every wicked act that is now done had not been decreed, its place might be occupied by one ten times as bad. We never hear of a deed of wickedness done, but we can conceive of one far worse. If the evil deeds then, which do occur, had not been decreed, their places might be filled by others infinitely worse.[7]

The model of divine permission has commended itself to a number of Christian thinkers. Augustine, for example:

> For of course, no one would dare to believe or declare that it was beyond God's power to prevent the fall of

either angel or man. But, in fact, God preferred not to use His own power, but to leave success or failure to the creature's choice. In this way, God could show both the immense evil that flows from the creature's pride and also the even greater good that comes from His grace.[8]

And Jonathan Edwards:

And, therefore, I would observe, secondly, they who object that this doctrine makes God the author of sin, ought distinctly to explain what they mean by that phrase, 'the author of sin'. I know the phrase, as it is commonly used, signifies, something very ill. If by the author of sin, be meant the sinner, the agent, or actor of sin, or the doer of a wicked thing, so it would be a reproach and blasphemy to suppose God to be the author of sin ... But if by the author of sin is meant, the permitter, or not hinderer of a sin, and at the same time, a disposer of the state of events, in such a manner, for wise, holy, and most excellent ends and purposes, that sin if it be permitted, or not hindered will most certainly and infallibly follow – I say, if this be all that is meant by being the author of sin, I do not deny that God is the author of sin, (though I dislike and reject the phrase, as that which by use and custom is apt to carry another sense).[9]

While Augustine and Edwards make use of the idea of permission, it is clear that they have specific and not general permission in mind, a permission which is in accord with God's having wise and holy ends which embrace every detail of his creation.

But is not the permission of evil itself an evil? And if God permits evil, can he avoid the charge of being less than all-good? It is by no means obvious that this is true, though if it is it would count against both general and specific permission, and create a problem for both the 'risk' and 'no-risk' views of divine providence. We shall investigate this matter more fully when considering the problem of evil in the next chapter.

Model 3: divine compatibilism

So far, we have looked at two models which attempt, in a direct fashion, to preserve the biblical datum that God is not the author of sin, while at the same time adopting a 'no-risk' view of divine providence. The third model which we shall consider proceeds in a less direct fashion.

Some, who hold the view that all human choices are causally determined by desires and intentions, also argue that such determination is logically incompatible with human freedom and responsibility. Other determinists are *compatibilists*, arguing the opposite, and this is the position adopted in this study as being in the greatest accord with a 'no-risk' view of divine providence. What the third model claims is that if compatibilism is true, the fact that it is God who ordains those factors which determine human agency, and that the factors are not determined in a purely natural or secular way, is not an *additional* difficulty for compatibilism.

The debate between compatibilists and incompatibilists is a perennial one, as is the wider debate between determinists and indeterminists. The model we are considering does not attempt to settle that debate, but takes one side of it, in the belief that it is not unreasonable to assume the truth of one side of an issue which is perennially debated. What it then proceeds to argue is that the fact of divine agency does not pose an additional difficulty for compatibilism (hence 'divine compatibilism').

The champion of this view among the theologians has undoubtedly been Jonathan Edwards. In his book *The Freedom of the Will* he takes the view that the human will is the outcome of motives:

> Let the person come by his volition or choice how he will, yet, if he is able, and there is nothing in the way to hinder his pursuing and executing his will, the man is fully and perfectly free, according to the primary and common notion of freedom.[10]

Edwards proceeds to contrast such a view of freedom with

174

the self-determining power of the will, to indifference and to the absence of causal necessity.

When faced with the idea of divine compatibilism, the view that God's determination of all events is nonetheless compatible both with human freedom and responsibility, many have been tempted to conclude that such determination turns God into a manipulator or puppeteer or hypnotist, who toys and plays with his creation for his own amusement.

Such comparisons are unfortunate. They suggest that the *purposes* that God has in his creation and providential rule of the universe are either sinister or less than fully serious. Such a suggestion can be quickly dismissed. Scripture informs us that God has high and holy ends in creation and providence, and there is no need to doubt this. But a deeper objection to such comparisons is that they offer ways of thinking about God – models of his activity – which are wholly inadequate.

Take, for example, the model of God as a puppeteer. This implies that his relation to his creatures is mechanistic; and though the divine puppeteer may be skilful, nonetheless the actions of his creatures are determined by pulling strings. They are not the outcome of their own reasoning processes, moral priorities and emotional responses. No doubt those who introduce the idea of God as a puppeteer or manipulator will protest at this suggestion. They will readily concede that there are no physical strings, and point out that men and women are not wooden puppets but minds and nerves. But whatever its rhetorical effect, such a model, however much subject to qualification, is fundamentally flawed. It fails to recognize one basic principle of Scripture, that men and women are responsible agents, which puppets clearly are not. We shall return to this matter later on in the chapter.

Many secularists argue that human freedom and causal determinism are compatible. But if they are correct, then things surely are no different if God is the determiner. This claim, however, has been denied, for example by Antony Flew:

> The situation is different in the purely secular case
> ... The difference is that in that case all human
> movings are supposed to be, not the movings at one

remove of the Great Manipulator, but the latest outcomes of ultimately impersonal causes. Whereas in the former responsibility must at the very least be shared with, if not shifted wholly onto, the supposed Great Manipulator; in the latter there is and can be no one else to blame.[11]

Why is Flew mistaken in this claim? As a compatibilist himself, he regards the crucial distinction – the distinction sufficient to establish human responsibility for an action – to be that between those actions which are performed voluntarily and those which are done out of compulsion. (The borderline between the two is extremely difficult to determine, but we may let that pass.) So it is only with respect to voluntary actions that the question of responsibility truly arises.

Flew goes on to claim, however, that if a person is caused to act voluntarily, not by impersonal forces but by another person, then the one who acts voluntarily cannot, under such circumstances, be free and responsible. So, given the 'no-risk' view of providence, it is impossible for men and women justly to be held responsible for their actions.

There is no denying the plausibility of the view that, if one person causes another person to act voluntarily, then that person bears some of the responsibility for what occurs. But this by itself is not sufficient to rule out the compatibility of the 'no-risk' view of providence and human responsibility, since it is evident that God does bear *some* responsibility for what happens in the universe that he has created. We may even say that God bears *ultimate* responsibility for it, since everything that occurs is ultimately due to him. This is true on any orthodox theistic view of God's relation as creator to the universe, whether deterministic or not.[12]

There is reason to think that in the 'no-risk' view of providence the responsibility for human actions is shared. Similarly, there would be reason to think that, if the causal forces bringing about voluntary human actions were impersonal, then such forces would also share responsibility for what happened. If the distinction between voluntary and involuntary actions still obtains in the case of determinism by impersonal forces, it obtains in the case of personal, divine determinism.

There is thus good reason to conclude that the 'no-risk' view of divine providence (assumed in this discussion because it best accords with the classical view of divine providence) creates no *additional* problems for the issue of free will and responsibility that are not already raised by determinism in general. If there is good reason to adopt the 'no-risk' view of providence, as I have argued that there is, then that reason is not weakened by Flew's charge. Alternatively, if anyone is concerned about the seemingly adverse consequences for human responsibility drawn from the 'no-risk' view of providence, it is to the compatibilism-incompatibilism issue that he should direct his attention.

Someone may think that in allowing that God is jointly responsible for the voluntary actions that people perform, too much has been conceded. Perhaps it has. But it is worth considering the implications of at least some of the alternative views of providence. If we suppose that, for example, men and women are not determined in their actions, but that God foreknows everything that will happen, then at the very least we may say that God knows what will happen for good or ill, and does nothing about it. Alternatively, if it is claimed that God restrains himself (restricts his own knowledge, for example) in order to allow for the presence of risk in the universe, then he is at least complicit in what occurs.

Thus on any view, whether taking a 'risk' or a 'no-risk' view of divine providence, it is hard to avoid the conclusion that God is to a degree responsible for what occurs in his universe. This, indeed, is what we should expect if the universe is created and sustained by God. More will be said on this topic in the next chapter, on evil.

Model 4: causal levels

Fundamental to any attempt to gain a measure of understanding of the relationship between God's activity and the human actions which take place within the order of divine providence is a recognition of the fact that God is the creator and that human agents are creatures. No model of divine activity and human action can ignore this and remain faithful to the biblical teaching. The problem arises, not with recognizing this fact, but with constructing a way of understanding that will do justice both to it and to the 'no-risk' view of providence.

We noted earlier, in chapter 3, the distinction between God, the primary cause of all that exists, and the various secondary causes of created things. One way in which certain theologians approach the problem of divine and human agency is to distinguish between two *orders* of activity, the divine and the human order. Thomas Aquinas, for example, draws such a distinction, in the following terms:

> God does act sufficiently within things as the first agent cause and that does not imply that the activity of secondary causes is superfluous; the one action does not issue from two agents of the same level; there is, however, nothing against one and the same action's issuing from a primary and a secondary agent. God does not merely impart forms to things, but upholds them in existence, applies them to their actions and is the end of all actions, as we have determined.[13]

Aquinas refers to *levels*. One action, say the action of typing this page, issues from two agents: it issues from God, and it issues from me. But these issuings of causal power do not compete or conflict with each other, because they are of different orders. Divine primary causation ensures the performance of the action of typing this page, from the point of view of the divine order, while my own causal power ensures the performance at the secondary level.

Among the Reformers, John Calvin makes a similar appeal:

> That difference of causes, on which I have before dwelt, is by no means to be forgotten – that one cause is proximate, another remote. The careful observance of this distinction is indispensible, that we may clearly understand how wide a difference

there is, and how momentous a distinction between the just and equal Providence of God and turbulent impetuosities of men. Our adversaries load us with illiberal and disgraceful calumny, when they cast it in our teeth that we make God the author of sin, by maintaining that His will is the cause of all things that are done. For when a man perpetrates anything unjustly, incited by ambition, or avarice, or lust, or any other depraved passion; if God, by His just but secret judgment, perform His works by means of such an one's hands, the mention of sin cannot be made with reference to God in those His righteous acts.[14]

The sun rises day by day; but it is God that enlightens the earth by his rays. The earth brings forth her fruits; but it is God that giveth bread, and it is God that giveth strength by the nourishment of that bread. In a word, as all inferior and secondary causes, viewed in themselves, veil like so many curtains the glorious God from our sight (which they too frequently do), the eye of faith must be cast up far higher, that it may behold the hand of God working by all these His instruments.[15]

It is by using this distinction between God the primary cause and created secondary causes that Calvin (for example) is able to distinguish between (a) human purpose and intention and (b) the higher purpose and intention of God in ordaining the action of the secondary cause.

Those things which are vainly or unrighteously done by man are, rightly and righteously, the works of God![16]

When God displays His power through *means* and *secondary causes*, that power of His is never to be *separated* from those means or inferior causes. It is the excess of a drunkard to say, "God has decreed all that is to come to pass, and that must come to pass; therefore, to interpose any care or study, or

179

endeavour of ours, is superfluous and vain". But since God prescribes to us what we ought to do, and wills that we should be the instruments of the operation of His power, let us ever deem it unlawful in us to sunder those things which He hath joined together.[17]

And a modern writer, James Ross, has written:

Employing Aquinas' principle that God is sufficient producer of all finite events, we know that in some sense He is the cause both of the sufferings and of the immoral acts of men. Yet we cannot think that He should cause these events in such a way that the acts of men would cease to be immoral, and the events would cease to be sufferings. God must be cause of my sinful actions in such a way that I still do what I ought not to do with full knowledge, forethought and responsibility ... Any interpretation of God's relation to the world which conflicts with that supposition is obviously false and contrary to those prevailing Christian doctrines to which the analysis is primarily relevant ... Our solution involves a proposition such as that of Aquinas: that for the same event two chains of causal sufficiency and necessity are simultaneously present, and simultaneously required.[18]

The Anglican theologian Austin Farrer argued that:

We enter into his [i.e., God's] action simply by acting, whether the action be a movement of thought or an employment of the hand. We believe and even claim to find, that his action sustains or inspires ours, but the divine assistance is experienced simply in its effect.[19]

The causal joint (so to speak) between infinite and finite actions plays and in the nature of the case can play no part in our concern with God and his will.[20]

Both the divine and the human actions remain

> real and therefore free in the union between them; not knowing the modality of the divine action we cannot pose the problem of their mutual relation.[21]

> Two agents for the same act would be indeed impossible, were they both agents in the same sense and on the same level.[22]

Farrer asserts the existence of the twofold level of causation, but offers no explanation of it since the exact relationship between the higher and lower levels of causation is hidden from us.

As explained by Vernon White,[23] this means that God so arranges and orders reality that whatever intention the creature has carries the divine intention in a wider context of meaning. Thus Judas' intention to betray Jesus carries a meaning within God's intention other than Judas' intention. This is helpful, except that (to preserve the two levels of causation strictly) we cannot say that *whatever* Judas intends is then placed by God in a wider framework of meaning, but that in some sense God causes the specific intention of Judas, and indeed of every lower-level causal event.

The two-level proposal seems to be a neat solution, and a persuasive one. It certainly has the merit of preserving the disparity between the action of the creator and that of his creatures, for it is wholly appropriate that these two actions should be regarded as actions of different *orders*.

If we look a little closer, however, certain difficulties emerge. Precisely what is the primary causal power from which my action issues? 'Issue' in what sense? Clearly it is not adequate to understand such issuing in terms merely of God's provision of *necessary* conditions for my action. For while the provision of necessary conditions would permit or make possible my action, such conditions would not ensure that it took place. In order to ensure that the action took place, the divine conditions, conditions in the primary order, would have to be both necessary *and sufficient*.

But if these conditions are both necessary and sufficient for the issuing of the action, then they ensure that the action takes place. If, though, there are divine causes which ensure

181

that this action takes place, then what part do a person's own desires and reasons (and whatever else we ordinarily think our actions issue from) play?

We can approach the problem from the other direction, from the second order, the order of mundane causes and effects. According to Aquinas and Calvin, my action of typing this sentence issues from me, the secondary agent. But then my desires and motives and other such factors (whatever in detail they may be) ensure that the action will take place. So what, in these circumstances, does the first order, the divine cause, play? For if my desires are sufficient to produce the action in question, why are the first-order causes necessary, let alone sufficient, for producing it?

According to this view, it cannot be that what God provides, by his first-order causal activity, is merely that I exist and that I possess certain powers. Rather, God acts in such a way that I actually employ those powers in the performance of a definite action. If I have it in my power (exclusive of whatever God might do) to perform the action, then the primary, divine causation can be only the provision of necessary conditions for that action, never a sufficient condition.

In summary, it is hard to see that there can be two separate sets of necessary and sufficient conditions for the same action, even if one of these sets is a set of primary conditions, and the other a set of secondary conditions. Calling certain conditions 'primary' and others 'secondary', does not by itself solve anything.

The significance of the models

We have reviewed several models or ways in which theologians and others have sought to order their thinking about the relationship between a 'no-risk' understanding of God's providence and human responsibility and accountability. But it might be objected that if, as we have suggested, some version of human freedom which is compatible with determinism best accords with a 'no-risk' view of divine providence, the only model that is necessary is model 3. Why bother with the others?

There are two reasons for this. One is that as a matter of fact many theologians, who have taken a 'no-risk' view of providence, have favoured one or other of these models. For instance, Augustine laid great store by the idea of evil as a privation. Secondly, while model 3 may be sufficient, it would not be surprising if features from the other models could be used to strengthen it. For the models are not exclusive of each other, nor are they the only models worth considering.

For instance, another model worth thinking about is that provided by Nelson Pike.[24] According to this view, God's omnipotent control is such that he permits creatures to have such freedom as will be consistent with his purposes, otherwise he intervenes. As Pike notes, this does not absolve God from responsibility. It also requires God to have knowledge of what his creatures will do before they do it, so that he can make any appropriate adjustments or provide additional assistance.

What do all these models show? As we have stressed, the reason behind them is not a scientific one, to explain certain events so that we may understand, predict and even control other events. Rather, the models are attempts to provide ways of thinking about God's relation to the universe which are non-contradictory, which remove obvious misunderstandings, and, most importantly of all, which do the fullest justice to the biblical data.

Readers may care to work out for themselves which if any of these models ought to be preferred, whether there are other more persuasive models, and whether or not any of them could be fruitfully combined together.

God's responsibility

Besides the issue of the exact relation between God's creative and sustaining activity, and the actions of his creatures, which we have been discussing, there are two main moral issues which arise in connection with God's relation to his creatures. These concern the responsibility of God, and of human agents. In our previous discussion it has been difficult to keep these separate. We are now in a position, however, to think about the charge that the 'no-risk' view of providence makes God 'the author of sin', in such a way as to compromise his righteousness. (In what follows I shall use the phrase in this sense.) Such a conclusion would be a grave and conclusive objection to the 'no-risk' view. But is it sustainable?

It would be unwise to argue that since whatever God does is morally right, it would be morally right if he were to be the author of sin. The problem with arguing in this way is similar to the problem encountered in Brian Davies's argument, considered earlier. Such a defence separates God from morality, either by separating his will from his moral character, or in some other way. The question is not what, in purely abstract terms, God or a god might will, but what the God revealed in Scripture might will. In the case of the God of Scripture it is impossible to divorce his will from his character. If, therefore, the question is, 'Could God, the God of Scripture, will what is morally evil because it is evil, in order to do evil?' the answer must, of course, be 'No'.

The claim that in a 'no-risk' providential universe God is the author of sin can be more fully expressed as follows. If God ordains whatever comes to pass, and there are morally evil human actions, then God is the morally culpable author of these evil actions. But the theist will argue that this is false. Indeed, if God is necessarily all-good, as he maintains, not only is it false, it is necessarily false. God could not be morally culpable for any moral evil that occurs. Anyone who wishes to maintain the contrary view must produce an argument to the effect that whoever ordains evil actions must be the author of the evil.

What might that argument be? Someone might claim that if one agent (God) causes another person to do a morally evil act, then that agent does moral evil. Whatever the evil that the agent (God) performs, he does not perform the evil which the person performs, since it is that person who performs it, and not God. Furthermore, whether or not God is guilty of moral evil is presumably a matter of what rule or law he has broken. But it is not obvious what law has been broken by God. Furthermore, it might be that the justification for God's action is that it is in furtherance of some greater good for which the evil act in question, assuming that it is an evil act, is a logically necessary condition. We shall explore this suggestion, and others, more fully in the next chapter.

Human responsibility

The maintenance of human responsibility is crucial for a Christian understanding of providence. Without personal responsibility for human failure there is no personal sin, and personal sin is an essential precondition of the very idea of redemption.

Two importantly different views of human moral responsibility can be distinguished. On the one hand are those who think of holding people responsible as a useful social practice for controlling and modifying the behaviour of criminals or 'deviants'. The issue of responsibility for them is a straightforward one: a person is responsible if the conditions exist for behaviour-modifying practices, such as blaming and punishing, to be effective. Otherwise a person is not responsible.

The second view of responsibility is concerned not with pragmatic, social effects such as these, but with the assessment of the moral worth of the individual. The basic question here is factual: irrespective of the usefulness of blaming or punishing the person, is that individual the one to whom the action is due? Did that person perform (in the relevant sense) the action in question?

It should be noted that each of these senses ought to be distinguished from the sometimes special senses of 'responsible' that arise in the law. In what follows no reference is being made to responsibility within the law, but only to personal responsibility, whether or not that is reflected in current legal and judicial practice.

The issue of responsibility is a subtle and difficult area. A number of complex issues come together: for example an agent's knowledge, the amount of control that he or she exercises in a situation; the agent's freedom from compulsion; the importance of what the agent is doing; and so on. Then there are the associated questions of the degree of responsibility, and the issues of blame and punishment. Should everyone who is blameworthy be blamed? Suppose that one person's action brings about some change, but only remotely so. Is that person solely responsible, jointly responsible, or what?

Both determinists and indeterminists agree that certain conditions are sufficient to remove responsibility. For example, each allows that if people are *compelled* to act as they do, then their responsibility is, at the very least, diminished. Each agrees that purely random occurrences, nervous spasms, twitches and the like, are also not actions for which an agent may be held responsible (though an agent may be responsible for getting into a situation in which the spasms occur).

But even these conditions raise problems. For example, take the issue of compulsion. There is a distinction to be drawn between external compulsion (as when one person physically forces another to act) and internal compulsion (for example, the activity of the drug addict). Then there is the question how a person came to be compelled; was it voluntarily, or involuntarily? During the time of the person's compulsion, whether external or internal, did he or she make any effort to fight it? If the compulsion is irresistible, does this exonerate the person if the irresistibility is one that the agent is unaware of, and that has never been tested?

Within the space available, it is not possible to do more than to state, and briefly to defend, a number of conditions for responsibility which are compatible with a 'no-risk' view of providence. The reader is referred to some of the more recent of the very extensive literature on this issue.[25]

We mentioned earlier the obvious fact that responsibility is a *causal* concept, and this provides a useful starting point. For one central issue is: under what conditions does the causal link between the movements of a person's body (or the absence of such movement, in the case of acts of omission) and the action justify the ascription of responsibility to that person? I shall discuss three central conditions.

First, *knowledge or awareness*. A person who brings about an action, but with no awareness (or a reduced awareness) of what he is doing, is to that degree not a responsible agent. If, for example, we are tricked into doing something or are unaware of any of the likely consequences of our act (as children and the mentally retarded often are), or if we perform the action when asleep or under hypnosis, such facts diminish our responsibility. Why is this? Chiefly because

actions have descriptions, and persons with a reduced awareness have a reduced understanding of the actual description
of what they are doing, what sort of an act it is (morally
speaking), and what its likely outcome is.

Obviously, knowledge or awareness of an action is not a
sufficient condition for responsibility. While I know and am
aware of hundreds of other actions performed by other
people, this fact does not make me responsible for any of
them. What knowledge does is to add a condition to the kind
of causal power that is necessary for moral responsibility.
The power must be power that is knowingly exercised.

Why is this important? Because it appears to be a basic
principle of justice or fairness that people ought not to be
held accountable for doing what they did not realize. Though
they may be held accountable for failing to realize something
which they had the power to realize. A person may be
responsible for firing the gun, but not for killing the woodsman, if he did not know, and had no reason to know, that
what he was aiming at was the woodsman. This is a condition
for responsibility that is commonly recognized both by determinists and indeterminists.

A more fundamental reason for linking knowledge and
responsibility brings us to a condition for responsibility
which, it has been argued, *is* sufficient for responsibility,
namely, *consent*. The sufficiency of consent for responsibility
would, of course, be denied by an indeterminist who would
require, in addition, that the action be performed by an
uncaused or self-caused act of the will.

Those who bring about some action, or fail to do so, must,
in order to be responsible for that action, *identify themselves*
with it. They must make it their own in the sense that it is the
action, and the sort of action, that in these circumstances they
overridingly want to do. Take the contrasting situations in
which we are unknowingly compelled (however this compulsion is to be understood) to do what we do not want to do,
and one in which we are similarly compelled to do what we in
fact want to do anyway.

The causal story is the same in each case; the line of
compulsion is identical. But the attitude of those compelled
makes a significant moral difference. In the one case they

187

disown the action as not being the action or the sort of action with which they wish to be associated, and in the other case they identify with it. Addicts may be willing or unwilling in their addiction. They might, or might not, identify with their addiction, and this will affect their moral responsibility for acting out their addiction. As Berofsky puts it, 'One may know of or acquiesce in a deterministic framework for human action'.[26] One may even, as Frankfurt has shown, be responsible for a state of affairs even if, had one not brought it about voluntarily, one would have been made to do it.[27]

Further, one may be responsible for doing X though there is nothing that one can do to prevent oneself doing X.[28] This is responsibility based upon character – the character that is exemplified in being willing or otherwise to identify with a particular action, even if that action is not only caused deterministically but also compelled. So the absence of power to do otherwise is not an automatic ground of exemption from moral responsibility.[29]

How relevant to our discussion are these claims about compulsion? It should be emphasized that it is not being argued that in ordaining whatever comes to pass in a 'no-risk' providential order, God compels everyone to act as in fact they do act. The distinction between acting voluntarily and acting under compulsion remains a valid one; and it is an important fact, about both freedom and providence, that the vast majority of human actions are performed in ignorance of what outcome God ordains for them. Rather, what these claims purport to show is that if responsibility is sometimes compatible with compulsion it is *a fortiori* compatible with divine ordination.

But in order to be responsible for an action on at least some occasions, should not agents have *control* over what they do? How is such control to be understood? It is at least the power to produce the outcome at will. A number of factors are involved in such power: the absence of compulsion (as we have already stressed), knowledge of alternatives, and knowledge that, by past experience, more than one of the alternatives are within one's power. It is not possible for a normal human being to produce, at will, the outcome of jumping ten feet into the air, and this fact is widely known. Hence a person cannot be held responsible for not jumping to this height.

The sort of power or control that is in view here is the power of the agents to do, or to have done, otherwise in a situation if they had chosen to do so; it is a hypothetical power. Had X wished or willed to do A, an action over which X has power, then X could have done A. But the fact is that in that particular situation, X did not overridingly wish or will to do A, and therefore did B.

Is this idea of control over one's actions compatible with a 'no-risk' view of providence? The sort of power or control in view here is the power of an agent in a given situation to do or to have done otherwise. Suppose that the situation is whether Jones should have ice cream or fruit salad for dessert. Suppose he chooses ice cream. Could he have chosen fruit salad? There are basically only two ways of thinking about the answer to that question. One is to think that Jones could have chosen fruit salad had his preferences, desires or intentions been different from what they in fact were. Such a position is consistent both with compatibilism and with a 'no-risk' view of providence.

The alternative is to think that Jones had, by his power of free will, the ability to choose fruit salad in exactly (exactly!) the same circumstances as those that obtained when he chose the ice cream. One may wonder about the rationality of such a choice. Even if rational, such a view of the will would seem not to be consistent with a 'no-risk' view of providence, since not even God could know the outcome of such a free choice.

As earlier, the reader may care to reflect further about the exact character of that freedom which philosophers and theologians who quite correctly say the 'risk' view of providence requires would have to be like. Some have held that such a view does not only fail to preserve responsibility, but is actually incredible.[30]

Providence and grace

One fact will have struck readers forcefully as they have considered the previous sections. The cast of the discussion has been centred upon the relationship between God's

189

activity and evil, particularly moral evil. But what about God's relation to human goodness? And, thinking of providence as it concerns the work and witness of the Christian church, what of the relation between the providence of God and *saving grace*? In closing the chapter we shall consider some of the issues that goodness and grace raise for divine providence in the 'no-risk' sense.

According to Scripture, there is an important asymmetry between acts of moral evil and acts of goodness. In the case of evil, whatever the difficulties may be of accounting for the fact, God ordains evil but he does not intend evil as evil, as the human agent intends it. In God's case there is some other description of the morally evil action which he intends the evil action to fill. There are other ends or purposes which God has in view.

In the case of goodness, God not only ordains the goodness, he is the author of it, not only in the sense that he ordains it, but in the sense that he is the cause of it. He intends it as such. As Anselm expressed it:

> God causes both the essential being and the goodness of all good wills and good works. And he causes the essential being of all evil wills and evil works, but he does not cause their being evil. For even as a thing's being is from God alone, so its rightness is from Him alone.[31]

There are two linked reasons for insisting upon this. One is that God alone is good, and that creatures have whatever goodness they have from him in a derivative and dependent sense. For this reason, though human actions are good when their intention and end are good, those who perform them can claim no merit for them. The idea of actions which in themselves merit the blessing or reward of God is foreign to Scripture and to the logic of grace. This is not only because scriptural ethics is expressed chiefly in terms of duty, and goodness in terms of a pure and single-minded intention and desire, but also because the source of goodness derives from God, and from God's grace in Christ. Hence, for example, the idea of acts of supererogation has no place in a biblical ethic, even though they are recognized in purely social or cultural terms (for example, in acts of heroism).

The other reason for maintaining that God is the direct cause of goodness is that saving grace as portrayed in Scripture is effective or effectual grace. This point is frequently misunderstood. Those theologians (such as Pascal in *The Provincial Letters*) who maintain that grace is efficacious are not making an empirical observation about the use and abuse of divine grace. There are many cases of grace being resisted, and of grace being far from invincible. Rather, they are making a logical or conceptual point, that while there may be varied workings of divine grace, some of which are resistible and resisted, God's purpose of *saving* grace is not finally resistible.

Such a view is far from being uncontroversial. Many hold that grace, however powerful, can always be resisted by the power of the human will; that God's intention to save a person can for ever be thwarted by that person's resistance. A separate book would be required to deploy arguments to uphold the position baldly stated in the previous paragraph. Nevertheless, it is for many an important beneficial consequence of the 'no-risk' view of providence, and of the compatibilism which coheres naturally with it, that it is congruent with the view that divine grace is effective or effectual.

The 'no-risk' view of providence, and the account of human freedom that goes with it, provide us with a way of accounting for the view that God's saving grace is effective or effectual. Those who wish to maintain such a view of grace while also upholding a 'risk' view of providence and the view of human freedom that goes with it, will have difficulty in doing so. For how can God's grace ever be effective if, at any point, men and women have the power either to refuse its onset, or to repudiate it after it has been experienced and enjoyed? Likewise those who wish to maintain that divine grace is always resistible have, in indeterministic views of human freedom, the resources to do so.

191

8

PROVIDENCE
AND EVIL

Many regard the central moral and theological problem of divine providence to be that presented by the occurrence of evil; moral evil, which arises as a result of human choices, and physical evil, such as storms and certain diseases, which occur apart from such choices. Such evil is said to be inconsistent with a providential order brought into being by an all-good, all-powerful God. We shall consider this problem, or rather this cluster of problems, in the light of the general approach to divine providence so far outlined, and the conclusions that have so far been reached.

The Christian will wish to address the problem of providence and evil with the biblical data on evil in mind. This requires us to reflect further on the nature of evil, and on its origin and character.

It is tempting to think of evil merely as a condition of human consciousness, a feeling of unhappiness, or as physical pain. If so, then goodness is happiness and freedom from pain. Others have identified evil with embodiment and have sought to lessen the effects of evil by abstinence and self-mutilation. But Scripture adopts a more radical view than either of these. Evil is personal. It is not to be identified with states of the body, nor with certain places, but it has its source, mysteriously, in the human will, in rebellion against God, in departure from his rule, in lawlessness (1 Jn. 3:4). The mystery is that those whom God created as good voluntarily defected from that goodness. And the mystery deepens when it appears that human evil is itself instigated by satanic influence. Christ called the devil a murderer from the beginning and the father of lies (Jn. 8:44).

Because evil is personal rebellion, it has the attributes of personal action. It can be intelligent and purposive. It supports itself with patterns of reasoning; it may appear plausible and persuasive; it flatters to deceive.

What, then, are we to think of the pain and unhappiness that are often thought to be what evil is? Scripture appears to teach that they are not so much the source of evil as its results, the evil results of evil. Viewed in this light, pain and unhappiness are 'natural' in that they are the natural effects of human rebellion, the effects on a human being of the rebellion by that being against its maker. They are also 'punitive', in that such effects are not prevented by God but permitted or ordained by him. It is the chilling teaching of Scripture that God may give evil people over to further evil (Rom. 1).

The 'problem of evil' is not an invention of the philosophers or theologians, but starts life as an acute personal difficulty. Its primary context is not calm reflection but anguish of spirit. It is the cry of Job, or of Paul – why me? Why am I, or why is some loved one, afflicted? Or it is the perplexity of the Psalmist as he saw the confidence and prosperity of the wicked (Ps. 73). Perhaps it is, less popularly, concern with personal evil and wickedness, a person's concern with one's own evil (Acts 2:37; Rom. 7). This is a central part of the problem of evil as far as Scripture is concerned.

Sometimes anxiety arises because of forgetfulness of the Teacher's observation that all share a common destiny (Ec. 9:2); and of the teaching of Christ, that the same sun rises on the evil and the good (Mt. 5:45), and that we should hesitate to pass judgment on those who perish in man-made disasters

(Lk. 13:4). And Christians today, like the early Christians, may forget that evils come to them as necessary fatherly chastisement (Heb. 12:5).

More particularly though, the Christian will wish to think about providence and evil in the light of who Christ is and what he did. For Christ was both the victim of evil – the Christian will say that his death is the paradigm case of the problem of evil – and also the one who came to deliver from evil. We shall need to keep all these matters in mind in the following discussion.

What should one look for in a discussion of providence and evil? In confronting the problem of evil we are confronting the basic enigma of our existence. It would be rash and impious to suppose that anyone can provide a satisfactory theory or explanation of why evil was allowed to enter the universe. A historical survey of the theodicies that have been offered confirms this.

But if an explanation cannot be expected, what can be? Perhaps it is possible to consider certain aspects of the relationship between divine providence and evil which will ameliorate the intellectual problem, and that will enable each of us to face it. This chapter has been written in this spirit.

In the long history of discussion of this issue it is possible to identify two main approaches to the amelioration, if not the resolution, of these problems. One of these, the free-will defence,[1] is already familiar to us from earlier discussion. According to this view, indeterministic free will is a necessary condition of human personality and accountability. In endowing human beings with such free will, and placing them in a created order where evil choices are possible, God brought it about that whether or not there is moral evil in the world is not up to him, but up to them, the creatures with free will. Given such creatures, God could not have created a universe such that they freely did only what was morally good.

We have also seen that there are two favoured ways in which it is argued that such an arrangement is compatible with God's providential rule. One way is to argue that God does not know what will happen, though he has expert beliefs about the course of the future. Such beliefs are nonetheless open to correction as human history unfolds and as men and women exercise their free will in ways that sometimes God himself does not expect or anticipate. We have argued that such an account of divine knowledge does less than justice to the biblical view of one to whom all hearts are open, and who knows the end from the beginning.

The second favoured way of reconciling human indeterministic freedom and divine providence is by an appeal to middle knowledge. This view maintains that God knows not only what he will do, but what would happen in all the possible circumstances in which people with free will might be placed. It is in the light of this knowledge that God actualizes that possible world which best fulfils his purposes. We have seen reason to doubt whether such middle knowledge is compatible, as is claimed by its advocates, with complete divine knowledge of human freedom and therefore with particular providence. But even if it is compatible, middle knowledge still leaves unanswered the question why God chose to actualize *this*, the actual world with all its evils, and not some alternative world in which the free wills of men and women bring about less moral evil than occurs in the actual world now. Even if middle knowledge provides a solution to the problem of the compatibility of 'no-risk' providence and human indeterministic freedom, it leaves the evil of the universe without an explanation.

In the conclusions to our previous discussions it has been argued that there are grave difficulties in incorporating indeterministic human freedom into a 'no-risk' account of divine providence.

We have also concluded that, while God ordains moral evil, he is not the author of it in the sense either that he is himself morally tainted by what he ordains, or that he takes away the responsibility of those creatures who perpetrate the evil (a responsibility which, we have argued, is compatible with determinism). In this chapter, therefore, we shall look at the difficult issues raised by the problem of evil from the vantage point of the 'no-risk' view of providence, which requires that men and women are free in a way which is distinctively human but which is nevertheless not indeterministic.

Some consequences for the problem of evil

This position has the following consequences as far as the problem of evil is concerned. Unlike those who appeal to indeterministic accounts of human freedom, it must be allowed that God could have created individuals such that they freely (in a sense of 'free' compatible with determinism) did only what was morally right. This is denied by the free-will defence, which claims that if God wishes to have creatures who are genuinely free, then he cannot ensure that any of their actions is morally right.

> There are any number of possible worlds such that it is partly up to Maurice whether or not God can actualize them. It is, of course, up to God whether or not to create Maurice and also up to God whether or not to make him free with respect to the action of taking oatmeal at time t. . . . But if He creates Maurice and creates him free with respect to this action, then whether or not he actually performs the action is up to Maurice – not God.[2]

But if we suppose some form of compatibilism, then God could have created men and women who freely (in a sense compatible with determinism) did only what was morally right. Why then did he not do so?

The answer can only be because God had a reason for not doing so. For it is not possible to maintain that he was in some way incapable of creating such men and women. But what sort of reason might that be? Presumably the general character of that reason must be *that out of that evil a greater good would come, a good that could not have come, or could not have been as great, if there had not been that evil.* But what sort of greater good?

Before an attempt is made to answer that question, an answer which will occupy the remainder of the chapter, two or three further clarificatory comments are in order.

At the beginning of this chapter it was mentioned that the problem of evil is in fact two problems: that of physical evil (earthquakes, disease and the like) and that of moral evil (those evils which stem from human decisions and actions). But while it is necessary for those who use the free-will defence to insist on such a distinction, it is less important for the greater-good defence to do so. For that defence does not, in the final analysis, attribute certain evils to the human will and certain others to natural causes; rather, all are finally attributed to the divine reason and will. So in what follows no sharp distinction will be made between moral and natural evil. Readers can adapt the discussion that follows to that distinction if they so wish.

In the second place, it is important to bear in mind that the free-will defence can also be thought of as a greater-good defence, though one of a peculiar kind. It is, in effect, a limiting case of such a defence. The free-will defence claims that a world in which there are human beings with indeterministic free will is a more valuable world (whatever evil might occur in the world as a result of the exercise of human free will) than one in which there are no such individuals. So God had a good reason – one to be understood in terms of the intrinsic value of certain kinds of actions – for creating such a world. But having created such a world, he cannot ensure that it has a particular outcome.

We might represent the difference in the following way. If the question is why God created a universe in which there is the possibility of evil, the answer of the free-will defence is: because God placed a particular value upon human beings with free will. And whether there is actual evil, as opposed to the mere possibility of it, and how much evil there is, is up to those whom he created. So endowing human beings with free will was a value with a risk attached to it – the risk of moral evil – a risk that God was prepared to take because of the value placed upon human freedom.

But the greater-good defence is concerned not so much with the possibility of evil as with its actual occurrence, and asks: given that evil actually occurs (evil which God could have prevented), why did God not prevent it, but rather ordain it? The answer provided by the greater-good defence is: because only in permitting evil (evil which God could have prevented by creating men and women such that they freely only ever did what was right) could certain ends be secured.

198

In Christian theology the question of the problem of evil is intimately tied to the question of the fall; of the creation of Adam and Eve, and of the relation of Adam and Eve to their posterity. This in turn raises questions about the status of the biblical account of evil. Is this history, or myth, or symbol? If it is history, what kind of history is it?

Some theologians sidestep this issue on the grounds that sin and evil are not transgressions against God but the inevitable outcome of the spiritual growth of the human race. They are signs of immaturity. We shall consider this view later on.

We are able to sidestep these important but difficult questions for a different reason. What concerns us is not the actual course of the introduction of evil into the universe, its aetiology, but the possible reasons for its introduction. Despite this, a little later something will be said about the place that the doctrine of the fall occupies in the problem of evil.

To make this clearer, let us suppose that the story of Adam and Eve in the Garden of Eden is literally true; there was a first pair, immediately created by God, a literal garden, a tree, a serpent, and so on. While such an account would provide an answer to the question 'How did sin or moral evil enter the world?' it would not provide an answer to the questions that are of concern to us. For the free-will defender would naturally suppose that Adam and Eve had indeterministic free will; the greater-good defence would make no such assumption. In short, any account of how sin began would be contentious in just the way in which we are attempting to resolve. A literalist account of the fall would not settle the issue, for each party would claim that account that was consistent with its own position.[3]

For this reason, our discussion will continue to be largely abstracted from any one account of how sin began. Readers should be able, without too much difficulty, to interpret whichever account of the beginning of sin they favour in either a free-will defence sense, or a greater-good sense. It is only where issues arise that concern the solidarity of the human race in moral evil that the details of the doctrine of the fall become relevant.

Why did God not prevent moral evil?

Given a 'no-risk' view of providence, God could have prevented evil by creating human beings such that they freely did only what is morally right. So God, being omnipotent and omniscient, chose, for good reason, not to create such creatures. Moral evil is 'unnatural', in that morally evil human beings are not truly or fully human, but its entry was not unexpected by God; rather, it was ordained by him.

This general approach accords with what several notable Christian theologians have said. Thus Augustine:

> For the Almighty God, who, as even the heathen acknowledge, has supreme power over all things, being Himself supremely good, would never permit the existence of anything evil among His works, if He were not so omnipotent and good that he can bring good even out of evil.[4]

So Augustine asserts that God would not have permitted evil unless he could bring good out of it. This is not quite the same as saying that the reason God permitted evil was so that he could bring good out of it. But perhaps there are goods for which moral evil is necessary. We shall explore this question later on.

Faced with the view that God would have permitted or ordained evil only for a morally good reason, there seem to be two further possibilities open to us.

One is that God has a good reason for permitting or ordaining evil, but that none of us has an inkling what that good reason is.[5] It is sometimes claimed that to take this position is to commit oneself to the view that God is pure will, and that what he ordains or permits is right simply in virtue of the fact that he permits it. This position is sometimes reinforced by an argument we considered earlier, that God is not a moral agent whose actions are susceptible to moral assessment by his creatures.

Since the God of classical theism cannot be morally

200

bad, the problem of evil cannot be used to show that
he is.[6]

This claim of Brian Davies's seems to contain an important
ambiguity. Because God is God and we are his creatures, it is
certainly improper (perhaps even logically improper) for us
to suppose that we could ever hold God to account. Nevertheless, the goodness of God's actions (that is, the goodness of
his character in accordance with which he acts) must presumably bear some positive relationship with human goodness, even if standards of human goodness are occasionally
corrected by appeal to divine goodness. Otherwise we are
faced with the old problem that what is goodness for God is
evil for ourselves and vice versa. Then what would it mean to
assert that God is good?

In any case there is no reason why it should follow that
because we are ignorant of God's reasons for ordaining evil,
his character is that of pure will. From the fact that we do not
know the reason God permits evil, it does not follow that
there is no reason. Perhaps, rather, we should *expect* a situation in which we do not know why God permits evil.

The other possibility is that God has a good reason for
ordaining or permitting evil and that we *do* have some idea
what this reason is: either because, on *a priori* grounds, we
believe that we know what such a reason must be, or because
such reasons are revealed to us, or for some combination of
these reasons.

We shall examine some of these possibilities shortly. It is
important first to stress that for any of them to provide a solid
reason for the divine permission of evil, the existence of evil
has to be a logically necessary condition for that desirable
state of affairs which follows from it. For otherwise God
would have ordained moral evil as one possible route (among
others he might have chosen) for that state of affairs which
he wills to bring to pass. The question would then be why he
chose that way of producing a desirable result, a way that
involved evil, when other ways not involving evil and suffering were open to him.

But is this correct? As the Bible presents evil, and human
reactions to it, it often has a teaching function; it is meant to

be instructive. This is so whether the evil is social inequity (as in Psalm 73, for example) or is more personal (as with Job or Paul). The awareness of evil is intended by God to teach those who are made aware of it certain matters which it is psychologically impossible, or very difficult, for them to be taught otherwise. So may the evil not be logically necessary, but merely psychologically necessary? But if the fact that Paul or Job needed to be taught a lesson is itself a moral evil, then perhaps after all evil is logically necessary for certain further goods. We shall proceed on this assumption.

In order for any version of the good reason or greater-good defence to be plausible on moral grounds, the evil (its character, amount and incidence) must be a logically necessary condition of the good that is alleged to follow from it. It must be that without which the good could not be achieved, not merely one means among others by which the good may be achieved.

But how should we know whether this were so or not? How should we know whether the evil had a contingent relationship to the good to be achieved, or a necessary relationship to it? One way would be to enquire whether evil enters *into the description* of the good to be achieved. This can be illustrated in the following way.

Suppose that the good to be achieved was happiness, the happiness of certain people at certain times in the future. One can define happiness – as a state of well-being or contentment or whatever – without reference to evil. Happiness is not necessarily an overcoming of evil or even a reaction to it. But suppose, by contrast, that the good to be achieved was *sympathy* or *compassion* or *patience*. These concepts are defined in terms of some supposed evil or lack or need which calls forth the sympathetic or compassionate response, and without which that response would not be intelligible. Of course what calls forth such a response may be what is *believed to be evil* by the responder. It may not actually be an evil. Nevertheless, it would be unintelligible to describe a response as compassionate or sympathetic unless there was believed to be an evil or a need to which the response was made.

Let us suppose, then, that the evils that occur are ultimately justified by the fact that without them certain good states of

202

affairs could not logically occur. One still has to ask, what is the (moral) justification for bringing about the goods? After all, the fact that certain evils are logical preconditions for certain goods does not, by itself, provide a justification for permitting the evils. All it says is that it is impossible to have the goods without the evils; not that the goods justify the evils. One must not confuse logical justification with ethical justification.

What possible ethical justifications are there, then, for permitting or ordaining evils without which there would not be certain goods? There are two broad and contrasting justifications. I shall refer to these as the *non-punitive* and *punitive* justifications. We shall shortly look at these in turn.

The greater good

Before we launch into a discussion of these contrasting justifications, it is perhaps useful to pause and consider the idea that they have in common. They share the idea of bringing something about, or allowing something to happen, for a greater good.

There is little doubt that the seeds of such a defence are present in the New Testament, particularly in Paul. Paul argues that the sufferings of the Christian church in this life 'are not worth comparing with the glory that will be revealed in us' (Rom. 8:18), and the light troubles of the present 'work' 'an eternal glory that far outweighs them all' (2 Cor. 4:17; see also 2 Tim. 2:12). There is here not only the contrast between suffering and glory, but also a connection between the two; suffering 'works' glory.

But a deeper relationship still can be discerned. Not only does suffering produce or work for glory, but the character of the glory, according to Paul, is such that it cannot be properly understood except in terms that presuppose sin and suffering. Sin and suffering, and glory, are not contingently or accidentally related, but internally related; there is a relationship of meaning between the two states. The character of the glory can be understood only in terms of the suffering.

It is a small step from here to the thought that those events which involved sin and suffering, and which were under the

203

sovereign dominion of God, were permitted by him, or ordained by him, in order that the 'eternal glory that far outweighs them all' should come to pass. For without such events the eternal weight of glory could not have occurred.

But what of the morality of the idea that God ordained evil that good may come? Is this not a case of the end justifying the means? We have already covered this ground. Such an arrangement would be immoral only if permitting or ordaining the means was itself immoral. And for this to be immoral God would have to be the author of sin, be sinful. Our previous argument has been that this is not, and cannot be, the case.

Even if the means, as ordained by God, is not immoral, there are cases, real and imaginable, where the means is disproportionate to the end. It might be said: granted, God's ordaining that a child should be born with inoperable cancer is not in itself immoral, and granted that evil is logically necessary for certain further goods, but was the ordaining of a lesser evil not possible?

This is the objection of Ivan in Dostoyevsky's *The Brothers Karamazov*:

> Listen: if all have to suffer so as to buy eternal harmony by their suffering, what have the children to do with it – tell me, please? It is entirely incomprehensible why they, too, have to suffer and why they should have to buy harmony by their sufferings. Why should they, too, be used as dung for someone else's future harmony?[7]

We leave to one side the remark about suffering buying eternal harmony – this is not a New Testament thought. What is the answer of the greater-good defence to the question of the justice of suffering children? We do not know all the facts,[8] and in particular we cannot rule out that at some future stage suffering children may come to see that what they endured was for their good.

This point about the necessary limitations to our knowledge is even more relevant in the case of what has been called 'horrendous evil', that is an evil of such proportions that it is plausible to think that the one who suffers it cannot, on the whole, derive great good from it. For some people it is not so much the fact of evil that is a problem, but its depth. Why are so many lives shattered? Can it be seriously claimed that God ordains horrendous evils such as blighted the lives of those involved in the Holocaust? Some have even gone so far as to say that the fact of the Holocaust has permanently changed the way in which Christian thinking about evil is to be conducted.

How can such evils fall within the scope of God's providence? It is tempting to do the work of God, the creator and judge, for him; but that temptation must be resisted. He alone knows the true worth of a life in all its dimensions. We are ignorant of the facts, not only facts about other people but facts about God and his purposes for them.

It has been argued that while no reason can be given why God should ordain or permit horrendous evils, nevertheless Christianity has, in its account of the future vision of God, a way in which we can at least explain how the blight of a blighted life can be defeated. And this is certainly a prominent New Testament thought. The 'light troubles' of the Christian are swallowed up by the weight of glory that awaits him (2 Cor. 4:17). As Marilyn McCord Adams puts it, 'a face-to-face vision of God is a good for humans incommensurate with any non-transcendent goods or ills'.[9] In this sense, all horrendous evils are swallowed up and defeated in the vision of God.

Perhaps this is so. But in order to meet the problem of horrendous evil head on, it would be necessary to be able to say that each case of such evil will be swallowed up and defeated in this way. It is to be doubted, however, that Scripture provides us with warrant to say as much as this. Not to say as much as this is to say that God does not love every created person equally. Does this not coincide with much else that Scripture teaches about the discriminating character of divine love? If this is so, then, as Adams says, many would be unwilling to enter such a world if they knew that many lives, perhaps including their own, would have evils for ever undefeated.[10] This is a perhaps unwitting echo of Christ's teaching that it would be better for some men had they not been born (Mt. 26:24; cf. Mt. 18:6).

So perhaps there is no *one* explanation for all cases of horrendous evil. Perhaps some are to be explained in terms of a greater good, others in terms of chastisement and discipline, and others in terms of judgment by God. Perhaps each evil contains elements of these. We shall now proceed to explore some of these elements in more detail.

The greater-good defence: non-punitive evil

Some have argued that the justification for the infliction or permitting of evils which are a necessary condition for the production of certain goods is simply that they produce these goods. The goodness of the goods produced outweighs the evils which are permitted. Evils are the necessary growth pains of the human race.

This is the so-called Irenaean theodicy championed by, among others, John Hick in *Evil and the God of Love*. According to Hick, it is not that humankind was created good and is now fallen, but rather:

> Man as he emerged from the evolutionary process already existed in the state of epistemic distance from God and of total involvement in the life of nature that constitutes his 'fallenness'. He did not fall into this from a prior state of holiness but was brought into being in this way as a creature capable of eventually attaining holiness. In Irenaeus' terminology, he was made in the image but had yet to be brought into the likeness of God.'[11]

So for Hick both pain, considered as a physical sensation, and suffering, may be a divinely created sphere of soul-making which finds its fulfilment not in this life but in the blessedness of the kingdom of God.

In considering the merits of Hick's approach, it is well to bear in mind the sorts of situation that count as 'morally evil'. They include individually morally evil actions, situations which make the exercise of any morally good actions difficult or impossible, and the prosperity of evil people and the adversity of the good.

There would appear to be different versions or strengths of a non-punitive approach such as Hick's. For example:

(a) The ethical justification for the permission of evil is that it produces in everyone equally benefits which outweigh the evil and which could not (logically) occur if the evil did not occur.

(b) The ethical justification for the permission of evil is that it produces in everyone benefits which outweigh the evil and which could not occur (logically) if the evil did not occur. That is, while not everyone benefits equally, each benefits beyond an 'outweighing threshold'.

(c) The ethical justification for the permission of evil is that it produces total benefits which outweigh the evil and which could not occur if the evil did not occur. These benefits are unequal and some people who enjoy them may not do so up to the outweighing threshold.

No doubt there are many other variants of the three possibilities given.

In Hick's version of this theodicy, the matter is made complicated because it is combined with a commitment to indeterministic human freedom. So, unless a theory of middle knowledge is advocated, not only is the exact incidence of many evils unknown to God (since they depend upon the exercise of human free will of which God had limited knowledge), but also (and more importantly) the character and incidence of the benefits are unknown, since that incidence also depends upon the exercise of indeterministic freedom.

To illustrate, in *Evil and the God of Love*, Hick defends universalism, a situation in which every single human being enjoys unalloyed divine favour and bliss in a life to come. But given indeterministic human freedom such a state cannot be guaranteed, only hoped for and encouraged by God, since it is logically possible that some may perversely resist the divine overtures indefinitely.

Given indeterminism, it follows that there is a cloud of uncertainty hanging over the actual achieving of any end-state that may be specified as part of the theodicy. But while Hick, a prominent proponent of this theodicy, is himself committed to indeterminism, indeterminism is not a necessary or intrinsic part of such an approach. It is perfectly possible to hold that evil is justified by the good that will result from it as men and women react to evil in a way which is compatible with determinism and which God can infallibly ordain and foresee.

It might be objected, however, that, since God is permitting evil that good may come, such a state of affairs is fundamentally immoral. For it follows that all the moral horrors of human history have as their justification that out of them greater good will come, or that it is more likely than not that greater good will come. In other words, all the moral objections to utilitarianism are also objections to this theodicy.

We have already suggested one general reason why such a charge is not applicable to God. In addition to this, the moral objection to the practice of allowing the end to justify the means is that one person may benefit at another's expense; that evil may be visited upon one person in order that some other person, who is quite unconnected with the first, may benefit. But suppose that the means and the end concern the same person as, for example, in the training of a child. A child may suffer pain as part of its training for adulthood; this is not usually regarded as being morally objectionable, since the same person benefits. This could be formulated in terms of a principle, perhaps as follows: *That no-one suffers more than is necessary for the production of benefits which, in the divine providence, are benefits for themselves.* If this were true, then the charge of immorality against the Irenaean theodicy would be mitigated, if not entirely removed. For on this understanding of the matter, each person would, in effect, be being treated as a child who experiences suffering and difficulty as a necessary part of the development of character, the making of the soul.

Even so, this position seems to face a number of other difficulties. One is the factual question of whether the actual incidence of evil in the universe appears to be consistent with this training or soul-making view. This is a matter that would require detailed empirical investigation.

The second, and perhaps more fundamental difficulty, is not philosophical but theological. It is whether the virtual elimination from this account of anything that might be characterized as *redemptive* does not make it incompatible with the scriptural account of the nature and justification of moral evil, at least if the Irenaean theodicy is intended to be the *sole* theodicy.

The greater-good defence: punitive evil

Evil could not, in justice, be wholly punitive, since punishment presupposes offence, and an offence is, presumably, a moral evil. But it could be that moral evil, evil actions flowing from human decisions, are permitted by God in part as a punishment for other evils. Augustine claimed this:

> Vice in the soul arises from its own doing; and the moral difficulty that ensues from vice is the penalty which it suffers.[12]

And also:

> But if you know or believe that God is good (and it is not right to believe otherwise), God does not do evil. Also, if we admit that God is just (and it is sacrilege to deny this), He assigns rewards to the righteous and punishments to the wicked – punishments that are indeed evil for those who suffer them. Therefore, if no one suffer punishment unjustly (this too we must believe since we believe that the universe is governed by divine Providence), God is the cause of the second kind of evil, but not of the first.[13]

This introduces an issue that was absent from the Irenaean-Hick approach to the greater-good defence, the issue of justice. Granted that God is not the author of evil, it follows that one reason he has for permitting it, though not necessarily the only reason, according to Augustine, is in order that his justice might be upheld. And the reason why some evil is ordained by God is for the punishment of that first evil. But why does God permit evil in the first place, since it

209

is presumably perfectly consistent with his justice that no moral evil at all be permitted?

It would seem that Augustine and those who think like him might have two possible types of answer to this question. One answer would involve a reversion to the free-will defence. For it could be argued that the reason why God permits evil in the first place is because the good of creatures exercising their free will, even when they exercise it in an immoral direction, outweighs any other good.

This is a perfectly consistent view to take, so far as this current topic is concerned, even though it is not one that is in accordance with the overall position taken in this book. It is consistent to suppose that God might permit acts of free will, some of which are evil, and then ordain other evils which are the punishments of these first evils. It is difficult, however, to see (except on the middle-knowledge hypothesis) how the punishments of the first evils could be in the form of free, morally evil acts, or even free acts of any kind. Perhaps the most consistent position is to suppose that God, in justice, punishes free evil actions by ordaining natural evils as punishments. The problem this view would face is whether it is consistent with the facts about the incidence of moral and natural evil in the universe. Perhaps it is impossible for us to settle this factual issue.

To say that some evils are explicable as the just punishments of earlier evils is not to say that justice is wholly satisfied by the occurrence of the punishment, any more than it follows that the blessings resulting from morally good actions are blessings that are wholly commensurate with those goods. (In any case, as we saw, it is a part of the teaching of Scripture that some of the blessings of God may fall indiscriminately on the good and the evil.) If this is so, and God is just, it would appear to follow that there must be an afterlife in which the moral inequities of the present life are righted, even granted that some of the goods and evils of life are rewards and punishments for earlier goods and evils.

The situation is made more complex by the fact that not only is there often disproportion, or apparent disproportion, between the moral evil of an action and a further evil which might be regarded as the punishment for the action but there are cases of evil in which there has been no opportunity for the person in question to have done moral evil. We have already touched upon the case of small children who suffer.

The second type of answer, an answer not involving any appeal to indeterministic freedom, might take a number of different forms. One response would be to appeal to pure divine sovereignty, but we have already seen the dangers of separating the consideration of God's will from his moral character. A modified version of this would be to appeal, not to pure will, but to God's right as the creator to do what he wills with his creatures. This is how the apostle Paul argues: 'Shall what is formed say to him who formed it, "Why did you make me like this?"' (Rom. 9:20).

Another response would be to appeal to our ignorance. Perhaps there is some morally-relevant factor in this situation of which we are unaware.

A third would be to appeal to human solidarity, according to which the moral plight of one individual cannot be considered in isolation from that of everyone else. As we saw earlier, it is logically impossible for all moral evil to be punitive in character, since there must be non-punitive moral evil which the later evil punishes. This fact, together with the idea of human solidarity in a first act of moral evil is, in effect, what the doctrine of the fall propounds; a first, cataclysmic sin which involves not only the first sinner but all who are 'in' him, the whole race.

As Augustine expresses it:

> Since, therefore, by the favour of Christ we are Catholic Christians: We know that children not yet born have done nothing either good or evil in their own life, nor have they any merits of any previous life, which no individual can have as his own; that they come into the miseries of this life; that their carnal birth according to Adam involves them at the instant of nativity in the contagion of the primal death; that they are not delivered from the penalty of eternal death, which a just verdict passing from one lays upon all, unless they are born again in Christ through grace.[14]

211

Here Augustine is obviously echoing Paul's argument in Romans 5.

Such a view has been criticized on two main grounds, one philosophical, one scientific. The scientific objection, which we cannot go into here, is that the idea of the fall is at odds with the findings of natural science, particularly with the theory of evolution by natural selection.

The philosophical objection, voiced by John Hick among others, is that the fall is logically inconsistent with the idea of an all-good creation. How, it is asked, if the creation is all good, can the evil of the fall arise in it?

> Men (or angels) cannot meaningfully be thought of as finitely perfect creatures who fall out of the full glory and blessedness of God's kingdom. Sin – self-centredness rather than God-centredness – can only have come about in creatures placed in an environment other than the direct divine presence.[15]

This seems correct. But while Scripture portrays the original creation as 'very good', it does not portray mankind as created in the full glory and blessedness of God's kingdom. It is interesting that someone as Augustinian as John Calvin maintained that mankind's original condition was 'weak, frail and liable to fall'.[16] From the fact that something is good, it does not follow that it is as good as can be. It is not possible to explain the origin of human sin,[17] but it is possible to say that it could have come about only by humanity being left to itself. For reasons fully known only to himself, God did not create or sustain those conditions which would have ensured that no sin occurred. Though the choice of a sinful course of action was wicked in that it was God-defying, this does not mean that such a choice is irrational because inexplicable. It may in one sense have been irrational, but it is all too easily explained.

For all the difficulties attached to it, this view has one overriding advantage; it has the effect of preserving the universe as a moral order in which evil is punished. According to the Irenaean greater-good defence, by contrast, there is no moral order to the universe. All moral evils are growth pains for an end-state which is intended by God but which, due to the vagaries of human free will, may never the realized. There is, at best, a moral end, but not a moral order.

The greater-good defence: *O felix culpa!*

So far we have highlighted two contrasting ways in which the problem of evil, as it affects the idea of divine providence, has been addressed: one in terms of human growth and development, the other in terms of strict justice. I shall argue that each of these approaches contains elements, albeit in a somewhat inchoate form, which can be combined together to provide a more satisfactory view of the problem of evil, and one which accords with the outlook of Scripture.

Each approach preserves an important insight which ought not to be lost. How can the elements be combined together? The first, the Irenaean approach, preserves the insight that evil, moral evil, is necessary for a greater good. The soul-making aspect of the approach maintains that without the occurrence of moral evil certain other goods could not, logically speaking, arise. Without weakness and need, no compassion; without fault, no forgiveness, and so on. This insight must be preserved.

The other insight, that offered by the punitive view, is that of the universe as a moral order in which justice reigns. This is surely fundamental to any Christian view of the universe. Earlier we have struggled to understand how God can ordain evil and yet not be the author of it. The reason behind the imperative need to uphold this position, whatever the difficulties of doing so, is that the universe is a moral order. The problem with the Irenaean theodicy is that it loses sight of this fact, claiming that any evil is permissible which has a growth-producing effect, or is likely to have. On the other hand, the problem with the punitive view is that it can offer no explanation of why evil was permitted in the first place. For while justice requires that, if moral evil occurs, it should be punished, it does not offer any justification of why evil should first occur.

It is possible to argue that in the work of Christ these elements, the punitive and the remedial, come together. For on the one hand the work of Christ is an act of justice. In Christ moral evil is punished. Christ's atonement is, as Paul argued, the upholding *par excellence* of the divine righteousness (Rom. 3:26). This view requires that the atonement be not only exemplarist, but substitutionary as well; indeed, exemplarist *because* substitutionary.

By the vicariousness of Christ's death those who have done evil are pardoned and then renewed. But both the concepts of *pardon* and *renewal* logically presuppose the occurrence of moral evil. For no-one can (logically) be pardoned who has not committed a fault; no one can (logically) be renewed who is not in need of renewal.

It is such points as these that are behind what is sometimes referred to as the *O felix culpa!* approach to theodicy. The 'happy fault' to which this phrase refers is the fall of Adam. This is happy because it, and it alone, makes possible the divine redemption from which the blessings of pardon and renewal follow.

In the bulk of our study of divine providence we have tried, for reasons of presentation, to keep separate the three contexts – the theistic framework; creation, fall and redemption; and personal guidance. But it is clearly impossible to separate these in fact, and nowhere is this more evident than when considering the justification of evil in eschatological vein. For here creation, redemption and personal guidance fuse together in redemptive re-creation and renewal.

In our account we have concentrated upon the strict logic of these positions, the logical fact that pardon presupposes fault, for example. But there is another, greater-good aspect to this which it is worth emphasizing. The state of pardon and of renewal is one of greater worth or blessedness than a faultless original position. Isaac Watts' lines

> In him the tribes of Adam boast
> More glories than their father lost

express the thought that not only was there strict justice in the atonement, and not only is there the prospect of renewal in it, but the states of forgiveness and of renewal and all that these imply are a greater overall good than a state of primitive innocence. So there is growth and renewal. Unlike the Irenaean theodicy, however, that growth and renewal have a moral basis, both in the moral character of the evil from which Christ came to redeem us, and in the moral character of the atonement itself.

There is one further and final aspect of this that ought not to be forgotten. Not only is mankind subject to logic, God is as well. As it is impossible for a person to be forgiven who has not committed a fault, so it is impossible for God to forgive, to show mercy, in a universe in which there is no fault. If one supposes that it is a good thing for God to display his mercy and grace, and that both the universe and its creator benefit if God manifests his forgiveness and grace, then this also provides a reason for permitting evil. That is, any Christian theodicy must not only have a manward emphasis but also, and perhaps predominantly, a God-ward aspect as well. In the permission of moral evil lies the prospect of God's own character being revealed in ways which, but for the evil, it could not be.

The following is a logically consistent view. Some moral evils are a punishment; some moral evils are disciplinary; some moral evils are perhaps both. But moral evils whether considered as punishments or as disciplines presuppose moral evils which are neither. In Christ, evil as punishment and evil as discipline are linked, in that his atonement is both the enduring of punishment for moral evil, and the source of renewal. Finally, without the permission of moral evil, and the atonement of Christ, God's own character would not be fully manifest.

The personal response to evil

The entire Christian faith might be said to be a response to evil. Certainly one's view of divine providence *conditions* one's personal response to evil, and in this way divine providence and human spirituality come together. The final chapter will take some of these matters further.

If we believe in a 'risk' view of providence, based upon an incompatibilist view of free will, or for some other reason, then there will be many occurrences in our lives which are as surprising to God as they are to us. In these circumstances, it will be impossible for us to see our lives as a response to what God has ordained, since on this view God has ordained only a proportion of those events which befall us, that proportion which does not involve the free choices of human creatures, and which those free choices in no way affect.

9

RECKONING
WITH PROVIDENCE

In this study we have been struggling with some of the deepest and most intractable problems in Christian theology: the will of God and the presence of evil in his creation. But there is another side to divine providence which, while we have touched upon it in the course of the book, we have not so far emphasized.

According to Scripture God's providential rule over his creation is a fact. It is intended to have distinctive, operational consequences for the Christian believer and for the church. God's providence does not merely set an agenda of problems for the theologian and the metaphysician, though it does that aplenty, but it is part of divine revelation. As revealed truth, it is meant to have practical value for the believer, for the one who is committed to belief in divine providence. In this closing chapter some leading motifs of the Christian view of providence are set out in an attempt to answer the question, 'How is the Christian to reckon with the fact of divine providence?'

This study has turned upon the distinction between a view of providence in which God takes risks, and one which is 'risk-free'. Partly for convenience of exposition, and partly out of conviction, the idea of God's providence as 'risk-free' has been emphasized. Another reason for highlighting this distinction is to cast into relief the different practical consequences which ought to flow from each view. So, consistently with the position taken earlier, in this final chapter we shall explore some of the consequences which are meant to flow from the 'no-risk' view of providence for those who believe in it. Once again, the reader who differs on this overall position can work out what different operational consequences the 'risk' view has, as we proceed.[1]

A 'no-risk' view of providence, if it is the true view, has consequence for everyone, since providence governs everything. But the consequence it has for those who do not believe it differ strikingly from those who believe that every detail of their lives is ordered by God. That is, if such a belief is carried through consistently.

We shall begin by looking at certain motifs which do *not* follow from the 'no-risk' view.

Fatalism or purpose?

It is sometimes said that if God has ordained every detail of every life this has fatalistic consequences. Individual effort, initiative and responsibility will be stultified, for since God has ordained the future, and God's ordination is all-powerful, then there is nothing that any of us can do to alter it. If he has ordained that I will be promoted, or fall ill, or go to Blackpool for my holidays, then there is nothing that will frustrate that will. On the other hand, if he has ordained that I will not be promoted, or that I will take a trip to Barcelona, then there is nothing that I can do about that either. So, in these circumstances, the rational course is either to be completely idle, or else to live in an irrational and totally unplanned way.

Certain Christian writers, such as Augustine and Boethius, have not hesitated to talk of 'fate' in connection with providence. To modern ears, though, the interchangeability of 'providence' and 'fate' has a curious ring to it. 'Fate' suggests impersonality, as in astrological beliefs; but providence is personal, the personal activity of God in his creation through which he brings it to its appointed end or destiny. Fate may also suggest the interference of the gods, whereas providence is the all-embracing rule of the one God.

But should 'no-risk' providence, if followed through consistently, produce inactivity, since whatever will be, will be? This is based upon a misunderstanding. For according to Scripture God does not ordain ends without ordaining the means; the two are inseparable. If he ordains the victory he must ordain the battle; if he ordains the battle he must ordain the army, and so on. The end that is 'fated' can then come about only via the means necessary for effecting that end. If it is ordained that I shall go to Blackpool for my holidays, then as likely as not this will take place through the normal ways in which holidays are arranged, even though, as with all human plans, some of the outcomes of my decision may be unplanned and unintended, and even unforeseen, and so 'accidental'.

Furthermore, living as we do in a fairly orderly world, in which we are able to learn by experience that certain events are causes, and other events the effects of those causes, it is possible to know innumerable basic facts about our environment. For instance, we know that if we heat the water then, other things being equal, it will boil. Of course much is wrapped up in the 'other things being equal'. Nonetheless, the fact that we live in an orderly world means that it is possible to plan and to behave rationally and intelligently in it.

So in ordaining the end, God also ordains the means which bring that end to pass, and I, as a creature within that causal order, play a part in those means. The part I play is not always the one that I *intend* to play, or am even aware of. Nevertheless my actions have consequences, whether always intended by me or not, and in performing those actions I am contributing to the total of the causal order called divine providence.

There is another argument that is relevant here. Looked at from one point of view, the course of each of our lives, in so far as it requires intelligent choice on our part, is a series of forced options. What do I mean by this? At every moment of our waking lives not to exercise a choice is to have a choice made for one, since the passing of each moment closes certain options just as it opens others. This is because we live our lives in time and in space. The opportunity of performing an action at 12.30 pm, passes when 12.30 p.m. passes. To be idle at 12.30 pm does not mean that at that time there is a metaphysical vacuum, that literally nothing happens. Rather, something else (not an action of mine) takes place at that time. Let us call this an in-action. Furthermore, that in-action, given that the universe remains orderly, has causal consequences. Whatever the song may imply, none of us can stop the world to get off it.

So there is an inexorability about the world we live in, an inexorability to which we contribute when we reason and act, but to which we also contribute through inaction. Thus at anytime hosts of events will occur, and either we will contribute to them by our action, or we shall contribute (in a more Pickwickian sense) by inaction.

What does this show? It shows that we are caught up in a causal nexus, or flux, of activity to which our activities, or inactivities, invariably contribute. So the presupposition of the classical fatalistic argument, that ends could be achieved independently of any means, is an unsound one. The whole causal order is against it.

Of course if the fatalistic argument had been sound it would have applied equally to a 'risk' view of providence. For if fatalism were sound, then it would apply generally to all views about the future, not only, or even especially, to the 'no-risk' view of providence.

So one practical, operational consequence of the 'no-risk' view of providence is that all actions invariably contribute to God's providential order, that array of events which he wills to bring to pass. This is not so with the 'risk' view, of course. Some of the actions on this view are *against* that order, and God has to modify his actions in the light of them in order to effect what he intends.

But a mere denial of fatalism does not do justice to the 'no-risk' view of divine providence. That view has positive virtues; in particular it makes it possible to ascribe a significance to the whole of a human life, to every detail, as to the whole of history. It is just *because* God's providence rules over all, that individual human actions have significance in contributing to the whole. Whether the events of one's life are ordered by one's own actions, or whether they are literally out of one's hands, in each case what happens has significance in virtue of the divine decree. We shall have more to say about this later.

Irrationality? Reasons?

It is sometimes argued that an order of causality, such as the order of primary and secondary causality that we have been outlining earlier, is incompatible with thought, reflection and rationality. For if my thoughts and their outcome in terms of my action or inaction are risklessly ordered by God, then is not my intuitive belief that my actions are predominantly the outcome of my thoughts, beliefs and desires an illusion? I believe something because I take it to be true; that's what belief is. And my belief, coupled with an appropriate desire, is what moves me to action. How can this be so if in fact my actions are decreed by God? How can thoughts and desires have independent significance?

Put differently, if I am decreed to have the beliefs that I at present have, how can those beliefs be related to truth and evidence in the way that they are normally taken to be? There are possible views of divine providence against which this would be a valid argument, but it is not a valid objection to the Christian doctrine of providence, even in its 'no-risk' version.

Suppose that the way in which providence worked was by physical, mechanical determination. Our beliefs and desires would then be a by-product of mechanics, and would not contribute in their own right to any results. Such a set-up is clearly incompatible with reasoning and the processes by which beliefs are intelligently acquired and changed. If I am physically determined to think as I do, if these physical conditions are sufficient for me to have a certain belief, then the relation between that belief and any evidence there may be for it is purely coincidental. I do not believe *upon* the evidence; instead, I believe, and there is evidence, but the two

221

are not related, since my belief is caused in an evidence-less manner.

The supposition that God's 'no-risk' providential order is an exclusively physical or materialistic order is an enormous assumption not warranted by the facts. It assumes a kind of theistic materialism. The biblical view is that a human being is a psycho-physical unity, that the mind or self or ego is not material or physical in character, and that it cannot be reduced to the physical or material.

But if my reasoning is an intellectual, mental activity, and not physical or mechanical in character, does this not imply that it somehow escapes the providential order? Such a difficulty arises only on one rather implausible assumption that reasoning, because it is intellectual or mental in character, is not causal. But why should not my belief, that some course of action is the correct one to take, be caused by my awareness (or lack of awareness) of evidence together with my desire to bring about certain changes, or to prevent changes, that a knowledge of the evidence, together with other factors, permits?

Purposiveness

Christians can be confident, then, that their lives, including their reasoning and willing, are part of the divine providential order. They also can recognize that that order is a *causal* ordering, with a final end or goal. What other practical consequences ought this fact to have?

It warrants a general reliance upon God, based on the fact that they, in common with all humanity, live in a world that God has made and upholds, and which he has not abandoned or become indifferent to. On this understanding of providence there is no place for dualism, or a basic polarity between God and evil, or God and nothingness. Dualism implies uncertainty as to the outcome of things; an everlasting, unresolved, titanic struggle. On the Christian view, however, and certainly on the 'no-risk' view, God is in control, even in control of the forces of evil and wickedness, as the book of Job reminds us. There are no surds in his creation, though why God should allow the fact, extent and power of evil is a mystery to us at present. The Christian can be assured that even evil is subsumed under the divine purposes, and plays an integral part in them. Does this take away the force of evil, does it flatten it, or remove the tragedy and waste that are its products? Not at all! The Christian has only to glance at the cross to be convinced that this is not so.

Ought anything to convince the Christian otherwise? For often there is a sharp disjunction between the view that God is in control, and the seeming chaos and meaninglessness of human lives, and human affairs in general. Is not this chaos a *disproof* of the Christian claim that God rules the universe providentially?

It *would* be a disproof if the idea of divine providence were an empirical hypothesis, if it were built up only out of a person's direct experience of life and based wholly upon it. But – unless one takes a very broad view of experience – providence is not founded upon experience in this way. Rather, for Christians, reliance upon the providence of God, and an understanding of the character of that providence, is based upon what God has revealed in Scripture, and is confirmed in their own and others' experience. A confidence in God's assertions and promises is part of 'experience', and so providence may be said to be based upon experience. We have many snapshots of the interweaving of divine promises and human awareness in the Psalms, in which what God has said and done functions as an interpretative framework for experience. As long as Christians are able to have confidence in these assertions and promises, then any seeming counterevidence that arises in their own lives or the lives of others, will not count decisively against their confidence. This is one of the lessons of the book of Job, and of the character of Abraham. It is the general character of faith not to be based upon the current appearances of things. Faith is not sight.

To say, therefore, that chaos and meaninglessness disprove the providential order of God begs the question. So could anything in fact disprove it? Well, if Christians had reason to disbelieve the assertions and warrants on which their trust in God's providence is based, then they would have reason to abandon that belief. So since, as we have seen, the Christian's belief in divine providence is not built up from personal

223

experience alone, it cannot be overturned by personal experience alone.

The experience of weakness

It may seem that our account of providence stresses the power of God to the exclusion of every other consideration, and so distorts the picture. Surely there is more to God than power? In fact, in considering the part played by the promises of God, and the fact that providence cannot be 'read off' from human experience, we have touched upon another theme, the part played by the experience of divine *weakness* in providence.

It is tempting to think of God as a Herculean figure, able to outlift and out-throw and outrun all his opponents. Such a theology would be one of physical or metaphysical power; whatever his enemies can do God can do it better or more efficiently than they. Given such superpower, then the 'no-risk' view of providence follows.

But Scripture does not teach that the doctrine of providence follows from divine power in this fashion, though certain theologians appear to have held such a view.[2] Just as providence cannot be derived in any obvious or straight-forward sense from experience, no more can it be derived *a priori* from the doctrine of the power of God considered in the abstract. For the Christian view of providence reveals not only the power of God, but his weakness also. What do we mean?

There is undoubtedly a sense in which providence manifests the power of God. Creation is an act of God's power, and the sustaining of his creation likewise. The eternal power and godhead of God are seen in the works that he has made (Rom. 1:20) and sustains. But there is also a sense in which providence reveals the weakness of God, and in which the providential purposes of God are furthered by that weakness.

It is not that God is weak in the sense that he could be overcome or corrupted; nor that God is capable of suffering or of anguish. Nor in any sense in which God's omnipotence or omniscience would be compromised. So how can God be omnipotent and nevertheless be weak? How can he be all-wise and nevertheless be foolish?

The clue to the answer is to be found in what Paul says about the preaching of the cross in 1 Corinthians: 'For the foolishness of God is wiser than man's wisdom, and the weakness of God is stronger than man's strength' (1 Cor. 1:25). Paul is here referring to the fact that Christ's cross which, though foolishness to those who are perishing, is the power of God to those who are being saved (verse 18). The preaching of the cross is a stumbling-block to the Jews and foolishness to the Greeks; nonetheless it is through the cross, and through the power of the cross, that God has chosen to display his power and wisdom (verses 23–24). Let us try to disentangle this by distinguishing three different assertions.

Nothing that Paul says here is inconsistent with the idea that it is by the power and wisdom of God that the universe was formed and is sustained. The orbiting of planets, the growth of trees, the raging of a storm, are all displays of power, as well as of wisdom and goodness, as Paul makes clear elsewhere (Rom. 1).

But there is another kind of wisdom and power in God. It is the wisdom and power of God seen in the cross. It is the wisdom and power of grace, condescension and self-giving love expressed in Christ. Such wisdom and power was manifest in a kind of weakness. Consider, for example, Christ's resistence to the temptations of Satan in the wilderness, his refusal to be a judge or a ruler, his repudiation of Peter's overtures to make him a revolutionary, his rebuke of James and John, the sons of thunder, for wishing to call down fire from heaven (Lk. 9:54:6), his submission to degradation and suffering, refusing help from Peter's sword or from the angelic legions of heaven.

What do all these reactions have in common? From one point of view they exhibit strength, from another point of view weakness. There is a kind of strength shown in refusing to become a world leader or revolutionary, strength in the repudiation of the values typically exhibited in such roles, and in the refusal of the ambitions that usually drive political leaders and revolutionaries. It is the sort of strength exhibited when a man negotiates with those who are armed while being himself unarmed and defenceless.

Of course such attitudes and postures are from another point of view, a kind of weakness. Joseph Stalin understood this when he exclaimed 'The Pope! How many divisions has *he* got?' In physical combat, the unarmed man is likely to lose; the person who repudiates the role of a revolutionary or political leader is unlikely to gain a following from the dissatisfied or from those with ambitions for success. In the normal means-end thinking that governs the activities of rational and intelligent people, political success comes from political effort, and it is foolish to hope for success from a cross.

Well, which is it; is the cross weakness or strength? Is it wisdom or folly? Paul's answer is clear enough; the cross is the power and wisdom of God (1 Cor. 1:24). When the preaching of the cross is refracted by an attitude which Paul calls Greek or Jewish, then it appears to those with that attitude to be either weakness or folly. But God has made foolish the wisdom of this world (verse 20).

So, besides the power that made the worlds and upholds them, God displays power of a sort that is discontinuous with that power, in that many of his purposes, his chief purpose, is not an act of military might, or political cunning. The power that upholds the physical forces of the universe provides the setting, the necessary conditions for the exercise of this other sort of power; but the other sort of power is not more of the same.

According to Paul, such wisdom and power is literally wisdom and power. It is not that the wisdom of the Greeks is literally wisdom, and the wisdom of the cross loosely or metaphorically or symbolically so. There is a moral or spiritual refraction which prevents all men and women seeing divine wisdom as such, but such it is. This is how God really is; God's moral and spiritual character is such that the cross is entirely congruous with it, and is perhaps (though this is more controversial) the only expression that divine wisdom and power could have taken when faced with the human predicament.

We see how inept (to say the least) it has been when men have taken the sword in the name of Christ and sought the advancement of his kingdom through its power, and that of the

226

rack and the thumbscrew, or through political cunning, or the power of mass psychology or the tricks of advertising.

How does this help us to reckon with divine providence? In more than one way. To start with, because of the central part played in the divine purposes by that weakness, signs of such weakness enable us to form judgments about the relative importance of things. For the purposes of God, the *telos* of the creation, can be explained only in terms of the wisdom and power of God just sketched. This emphasis upon divine weakness should correct any idea that Christian believers' convictions about divine providence, with its stress on divine control, manifests on their part a hunger for power or the worship of naked power or sovereignty. The humbling and death of Christ is part of that divine providential order, and yet what that manifests is not the naked strength of God but (in the eyes of some at least) abject weakness and folly.

The judgments that the Christian makes about what is significant in life are not infallible, of course, but they are nevertheless *informed*. One can make such judgments at the micro or the macro level. Which is more important, the Reformation or the widespread use of gunpowder? Or which is more important, a person's popularity or his adherence to the way of the cross?

What Paul calls the power and wisdom of God are not equivalent to sheer literal powerlessness or folly. They are not bumbling incompetence, but a different *kind* of power and wisdom. So this power and wisdom are still effective in bringing about certain ends. The power of the cross is effective in the creation of the church and her preservation in time, and in her ultimate glorification.

Just as it is mistaken to identify the power of God exclusively with the power to bring the worlds into being and to keep them there, so it is equally mistaken to equate the power of God with any political programme, whether it be the rise of Nazi Germany or of the British Empire or the plight of the Third World poor. It does not follow that because the power of God is not to be exhaustively understood in terms of metaphysical power, any instance of human weakness exemplifies the power of God. It is mistaken to claim, therefore, that the power of God is seen manifested through what

Gutiérrez refers to as 'the power of the poor in history'.[3] Because God's power is sometimes, and most distinctively expressed, in weakness, it does not follow that any expression of weakness is an expression of the power of God. The poverty of such poor, the economically impoverished, is still a political category, a category in which the familiar dialectics of human politics makes sense. To suppose that such poor, simply in virtue of their poverty, are not corrupted by self-interest[4] is sheer sentimentality.

So the 'weakness' of God is power, the power of God to salvation as Paul elsewhere puts it (Rom. 1:16), and it has the power of God as its presupposition. This is clear from a crucial text that we have referred to a number of times – Acts 2:23. Christ was delivered up to the hands of wicked men, to humiliation and degradation, by the determinate counsel and foreknowledge of God. That is, such a delivering up was part of the providential order, and God's sustaining and directing power was necessary in order to bring it to pass. Yet the act itself, the offering up of the eternal Son of God, was an action that, by conventional human reckoning, was an act of weakness and humiliation.

So the confidence that the believer has in God's sovereign rule over all details of the universe is not confidence in naked force; it is not power-worship, a kind of spiritual fascism. Rather, it is confidence that is based upon the promises of God as these are made good in Christ. It is through Christ that men and women are able to have confidence in God. This sort of confidence is not that of worldly success or triumph, but confidence in ultimate reconciliation and righteousness in God's kingdom, which is the *telos* of God's providential rule.

So a second way in which the character of God's providence is important is in its consequences for the personal experience of spiritual weakness. Such an experience is not a sign of God-forsakenness, but rather the reverse.

Providence and ignorance of God's purposes

Just as the Christian's confidence of God is not based upon the naked power of God, so it is not based upon an intimate knowledge of the future course of God's providential purposes. There is a popular misconception that because a person affirms that God has purposes which extend to every event of the universe, the one who makes such an affirmation has an insight into or knowledge of these. But this does not follow even in the case of human plans, much less in the case of the divine plan. The fact that I know that you have a plan for decorating the lounge does not mean that I know what that plan is; even more so with the divine plan.

Even if a Christian has millennial expectations of a certain sort, these must in the nature of the case be so vague that their operational consequences are correspondingly vague. Certain views may incline to optimism about the course of human affairs, certain others to pessimism. Some historians have claimed that such attitudes have had deep consequences for culture; they have linked postmillennialism with American cultural optimism, the 'American Dream', for example. Even if they are correct in this view, such a general feeling of optimism does not of itself constrain choice very directly.

Paradoxically, it is the very ignorance of the detail of the divine plan which contributes to its fulfilment. Were we to know what God had planned for us then one of two possibilities seems likely. It is likely either that a principle of counter-suggestability would operate, or that we would experience psychological coercion or pressure to do what we did not want to do. One of the things that being free (in a sense that is compatible with determinism) means is that the prediction of what I will do, when communicated to me, is an additional factor which relevantly affects my choice. It is for this reason that some writers have argued that there is not merely a psychological difficulty about predicting what people will do and telling them, but a logical difficulty.[5]

But if there is a difficulty, there is also advantage. Not knowing the future in detail, people are free, psychologically and ethically free, to behave in a responsible way. We are ethically free, in the sense that we are free to do what we believe we ought to do. The fact that we are ignorant of how our actions will turn out is neither here nor there. We do know, though, that our actions are part of a causal order and will not have effects that put God's purposes at risk, but will in fact further them.

We are also psychologically free; our ignorance of the future means that we are not constrained to bring about that outcome by a belief that the outcome will have some determinate form. This means that we can make up our minds about what to do freed from any constraints from knowledge about what we will in fact do.

So there is ignorance, perhaps necessary ignorance. This does not mean that confidence in the providence of God, coupled with such ignorance, is irrational. For the Christian, the rationality of such a stance is founded upon confidence in the promises of God.

What precise difference then, does belief in the providence of God make to Christians if they have no special insight into the unfolding course of events? It has this difference, that Christians can be confident that everything that happens to them does so by the divine will. Such a view may bring anguish; the cry to God of one who asks why he has brought about this difficulty or that setback. But it will also bring about assurance in God's wisdom and goodness to work all things together for good no matter how dark things may at present seem.

Other views of providence cannot say this, and will, if followed through consistently, generate a different kind of spirituality. For on the 'risk' view of providence what happens may be the result of human free will, either not foreseen by God, or the result in turn of some generalized divine permission. Such a belief would make for chronic uncertainty, in that the believers are never in a position to know by what agency what occurs in their lives has been produced, whether by the agency of God, or by some other agency because God has chosen to take a risk.

Providence and encountering evil

We have stressed that while belief in providence does not provide a way to unlock the secrets of the future, it nevertheless does provide an interpretative framework for one's own life and the lives of one's fellows. Nowhere is this clearer, or more necessary, than in the case of one's encounter with evil. When experiencing evil, whether physical pain or one's own follies or the injustice of others, the temptation is to despair and to distort.

To despair by thinking that the evil, because it is evil, is purposeless and in this way to despair of oneself or of others. To think of evil exclusively in terms of being *overcome*; distracted from one's own purposes, weakened or corrupted. There is no doubt that evil has all these effects. But the one who believes in the all-controlling purposes of God, while experiencing these effects, is able to understand them differently. Belief in providence does not promote masochism, nor give any countenance to the idea, sponsored by the Christian Scientists, that there is no such thing as physical pain. The Christian's pain and anguish are as real as anyone's. But belief in providence enables Christians to put their pain in a different setting.

How? By recognizing that the evil that they and others experience has been *sent*. It is not the result of a free-action of human beings who are temporarily outside the sovereign control of God; it is not the result of a basic dualism between God and evil that afflicts the universe, as the Manichees and other dualists have believed. The evil that is being experienced is the result of the sovereign will of God. While the reality of the secondary causes, the immediate causes of the evil, is recognized, the evil comes from God, not *as* evil, the vindictive affliction of a malicious tormentor, but from one all of whose ways are just and good.

Not only can Christians believe, in general, that the evil is not purposeless, or the result of divine powerlessness or inactivity, but they also have some inkling as to the purpose of that evil. They know, if they are thinking about evil as it affects them as Christians, that it is for their good. The exact nature of that good depends upon how they react to the evil. If they react to it in a rebellious or unresponsive frame of mind, then 'the good' that they will experience as a result of the evil will be different from that which they experience if they recognize that the evil may be a spur or a chastisement. But however they react to it, Christians can rest assured that the evil is part of the 'all things' which work together for their good, to further their conformity to the image of Christ.

The further away the evil that they learn of is from their own experience, the less assured Christians can be that they understand why it has occurred. But even here they can believe that the evil has a definite purpose, that it was not sent without a reason, a reason which is wholly consistent with the love and justice and wisdom of God.

Providence and overcoming evil

We have seen that a belief in 'no-risk' providence ought not, like fatalism, to encourage passivity. It is mistaken to infer that because God has ordained all that comes to pass nothing that we do contributes in any way to the result. There are other ways of reasoning which may be equally tempting, but which are unwarranted. One is to suppose that because the present world, in all its detail, has come about by divine providence, that everything is as it should be; whatever is, is right, what we earlier called *immobilism*. The other is to suppose that our present world, whether thought of either in personal or social terms, demands change; whatever is, is wrong, or largely wrong; this is *mobilism*. And of course there is an indefinite number of attitudes to providence in between these two extremes.

But providence, as such, is mute, and we should be deaf to any message that we may think it is transmitting to us. Providence does not call upon men and women either to be mobilists or to be immobilists. How then does providence link with change and, in particular, with overcoming evil in the world?

The clue to the answer to this question lies in the distinction, noted earlier, between what God commands and what he ordains, a distinction which it is necessary to make not only on the 'no-risk' view, but on almost any view. In his wisdom God ordained the cross, but he did not, and could not, as a co-conspirator have commanded people to crucify Christ. This distinction is relevant in considering the overcoming of evil.

Any desire for change, or for resistance to change, must be conditioned by two considerations. The first is what God has commanded, the divinely-warranted moral and social standards that he requires people to follow. These — whether considered in terms of the Decalogue, or of Christ's and the apostles' teaching — are of three kinds. Certain matters are *required* of us, certain matters are *forbidden* to us, and certain matters are *permitted*. Thus we are forbidden to tell lies, required to honour our parents, and permitted to wear red socks. Such requirements form the structure of what, in any situation, we are to do, what we are to seek to change, and what to maintain.

So the first question is, is some course of action an instance of doing what God requires, or what God forbids, or what he permits? But this is not all. If this were all, then the task of Christian ethics would be much easier than it is.

Each situation to which we may seek to apply these standards is usually complex. There are questions about our own powers and responsibilities, and those of others (is this my job, or is it the headmaster's?); questions about exactly what the facts of the situation are (were they serious, or did they say it as a joke?); questions about short and longer term considerations; and so on and on. In other words any situation involves judgment or evaluation, its assessment in the light of the facts and of accepted ethical standards.

To follow up these matters would require us to stray into other territory. They are difficult issues, over which Christians (and others) may profoundly disagree. The main point, however, is that a 'no-risk' view of providence does not exempt anyone from making such judgments in as careful a way as possible, and then holding to them conscientiously and courageously.

But such a view of providence should prevent us from trying to second-guess God. For one thing that our study of providence has taught us is that this is God's world. It is therefore folly to attempt to take the ultimate responsibility of it from him. When we have, by our lights, done our duty, then the consequences of our actions, for good or ill, must be left in his hands.

Notes

Chapter 1

[1]*City of God*, trans. Demetrius B. Zema SJ and Gerald G. Walsh SJ (*Fathers of the Church*, vol. 8) (Washington DC: Catholic University of America Press, 1950), V.9.

[2]Ulrich Zwingli, 'On the Providence of God', in *On Providence and Other Essays*, ed. S. M. Jackson and W. J. Hinke (Durham, NC: Labyrinth Press, 1983).

[3]I have tried to answer this difficulty in *Eternal God* (Oxford: Clarendon Press, 1988).

[4]Langdon Gilkey, 'Cosmology, Ontology, and the Travail of Biblical Language', *Journal of Religion*, 11, 1961, pp. 194–205. Reprinted in Owen C. Thomas, ed., *God's Activity in the World: The Contemporary Problem* (Chico, California: Scholars Press, 1983). (The quotation is taken from p. 32 of the reprint).

[5]'How to Think about Divine Action', in *Divine Action*, ed. Brian Hebblethwaite and Edward Henderson (Edinburgh: T. and T. Clark, 1990), p. 68. I am indebted to Alston for several of the matters discussed here.

Chapter 2

[1]The idea of risk as a central motif in Christian theology is to be

found, for example, in *The Divine Risk*, ed. Richard Holloway (London: Darton, Longman and Todd, 1990).

[2]In *God, Time and Knowledge* (Ithaca: Cornell University Press, 1989), William Hasker offers reasons for objecting to this. According to him God's knowledge of future events is derived from the actual occurrence of those events (p. 197). If this point were to be granted then God's knowledge would simply 'record' (by anticipating) the events known, including, presumably, his own frustrated attempts to change human wills. Would this mean that God has knowledge of some of his own actions only after he has carried them out, that he could not anticipate the effects his actions would have? If so, this would appear to be incompatible with his omniscience. As Hasker says, such foreknowledge would be useless. The reader must judge whether this view does justice to such scriptural statements of divine foreknowledge as Rom. 8:29; 11:2; 1 Pet. 1:2.

[3]*Ibid.*, p. 197.

[4]J. R. Lucas, *The Future* (Oxford: Blackwell, 1989), p. 233.

[5]Robert Merrihew Adams, 'Middle Knowledge and the Problem of Evil', in *The Problem of Evil*, ed. Robert Merrihew Adams and Marilyn McCord Adams (Oxford: Oxford University Press, 1990), p. 125.

[6]Richard Swinburne, *The Coherence of Theism* (Oxford: Clarendon Press, 1977), p. 176.

[7]Thomas Aquinas, *Providence and Predestination*, trans. R. W. Mulligan (Chicago: Regnery, 1953), p. 44.

[8]Vatican I, Session III. Quoted from Denzinger, *Sources of Catholic Dogma* (St Louis and London: B. Herder Book Company, 1957), p. 443.

[9]Westminster Confession of Faith (1647), V.1.

[10]R. Swinburne, *op. cit.*, p. 175.

[11]*Ibid.*, p. 176.

[12]*City of God*, trans. Gerald G. Walsh SJ and Grace Monahan OSU (*Fathers of the Church*, vol. 14) (Washington DC: Catholic University of America Press, 1952), XII. 19.

[13]Thomas Aquinas, *Summa Theologiae*, Ia. 14. 9.

[14]John Calvin, *Institutes of the Christian Religion*, I, 17, 12.

[15]R. Swinburne, *op. cit.*, p. 177.

[16]William James, *The Will to Believe and Other Essays in Popular Philosophy* (New York: Longmans, 1897), pp. 180–181. See also P. T. Geach, *Providence and Evil* (Cambridge, 1977), p. 58.

[17]*Institutes* I, 17, 13. Compare Aquinas: 'To speak of God as repenting is to use the language of metaphor. Men are said to repent when they do not carry out what they threatened to do' (*Summa Theologiae* Ia. 19. 7).

[18]See Alvin Plantinga, *The Nature of Necessity* (Oxford: Clarendon Press, 1974), ch. IX.

[19]William Lane Craig, *The Only Wise God* (Grand Rapids, Michigan: Baker, 1987), p. 135.

[20]A. Plantinga, *op. cit.*, p. 173.

[21]William Lane Craig, *op. cit.*, p. 143.

[22]William Hasker, *God, Time and Knowledge*, p. 52.

[23]On this, and much more criticism in detail of Molinist middle knowledge, see Richard M. Gale *On the Nature and Existence of God* (Cambridge: Cambridge University Press, 1991), ch. 4.

[24]For further discussion, see Luis de Molina, *On Divine Foreknowledge* (Part IV of the *Concordia*), trans. Alfred J. Freddoso (Ithaca: Cornell University Press, 1988). Middle knowledge is also defended by Thomas P. Flint 'Two Concepts of Providence', in *Divine and Human Action*, ed. T. V. Morris (Ithaca, Cornell University Press, 1988). It is criticized by William Hasker, *God, Time and Knowledge*, and by Robert Merrihew Adams, 'Middle Knowledge and the Problem of Evil'. There are other proposed solutions to the problem of God's knowledge and human indeterministic freedom, but they tend to focus upon God's knowledge as distinct from his will, and so are less relevant to divine providence. See, for example, Alvin Plantinga 'On Ockham's Way Out', in *The Problem of Evil*, ed. M. M. Adams and R. M. Adams (Oxford: Oxford University Press, 1990).

[25]J. I. Packer, *Evangelism and the Sovereignty of God* (Leicester: Inter-Varsity Press, 1961), pp. 18–19.

[26]*Ibid.*, p. 23.

[27]*Ibid.*, p. 24.

[28]*Ibid.*, p. 21.

[29]For further discussion of compatibilism, see Paul Helm, *Eternal God* (Oxford: Clarendon Press, 1988), ch. 9.

Chapter 3

[1]*Confessions*, trans. Henry Chadwick (Oxford: Oxford University Press, 1991), XI. V, p. 225.

[2]*Theodicy*, ed. Austin Farrer (London: Routledge, 1952), para. 27.

[3]Maurice Wiles, *God's Action in the World* (London: SCM Press, 1986).

[4]*Ibid.*, p. 29.

[5]'Providence and Divine Action', *Religious Studies*, 1978, p. 235.

[6]See *e.g.*, Richard Swinburne, *The Coherence of Theism*, ch. 12.

[7]Nicholas Malebranche, *The Search After Truth* (1712), trans. J. M. Lennon and P. J. Olscamp (Columbus, Ohio: Ohio State University Press, 1980), p. 449. A modern and sophisticated defence of occasionalism can be found in two papers by Jonathan L. Kvanvig and Hugh J. McCann, 'Divine Conservation and the Persistence of the World', in *Divine and Human Action*, ed. Thomas V. Morris, and 'The Occasionalist

Proselytizer', in *Philosophical Perspectives* 5, *Philosophy of Religion*, 1991, ed. James E. Tomberlin (Atascadero, California: Ridgeview Publishing Company, 1991).

[8]Nicholas Malebranche, *op. cit.*, p. 225.

[9]*The Great Christian Doctrine of Original Sin Defended* (1758), IV. 3.

[10]Thomas Aquinas, *Summa Theologiae* vol. 5, trans. Thomas Gilby (London: Eyre and Spottiswoode, 1967), Ia. 22. 3.

[11]*Ibid.*, Ia. 23. 5.

[12]*The Secret Providence of God* (1558), trans. Henry Cole, in *Calvin's Calvinism* (London: Sovereign Grace Union, 1927), p. 231.

[13]The Westminster Confession of Faith, III. 1.

[14]For a helpful treatment of this aspect of providence, see G. C. Berkouwer, *The Providence of God* (Eng. trans., Grand Rapids: Eerdmans, 1952), ch. III.

[15]Thomas Aquinas, *op. cit.*, Ia. 19. 2.

Chapter 4

[1]*The Open Mind and Other Essays* (Leicester: Inter-Varsity Press, 1988), p. 189.

Chapter 5

[1]William James, *The Will to Believe and Other Essays in Popular Philosophy* (New York: Longman, 1897), pp. 180–181.

[2]Such a view is set out by D. J. Bartholemew in *God of Chance* (London: SCM Press, 1984), especially pp. 94, 101, 138.

[3]D. M. MacKay, *Science, Chance, and Providence* (Oxford: Oxford University Press, 1978), p. 30.

[4]D. J. Bartholemew, *op. cit.*, p. 25.

Chapter 6

[1]Vincent Brümmer, *What Are We Doing When We Pray?* (London: SCM Press, 1984), pp. 5–6. Professor Brummer has developed these views further in *Speaking of a Personal God* (Cambridge, Cambridge University Press, 1992).

[2]Vincent Brümmer, *op. cit.*, pp. 46–47.

[3]*The Importance of What We Care About* (Cambridge: Cambridge University Press, 1988), p. ix. In a number of the papers collected in this volume, Frankfurt plausibly argues that causation is largely irrelevant to the issue of personal freedom and responsibility. What is of much more importance in Frankfurt's view is the structure of a person's preferences.

[4]*City of God*, V. 10.

Chapter 7

[1]Unless indicated to the contrary, in the remainder of the book 'free' refers to any of those senses of the term in which it is compatible with some form of determinism.

[2]Alvin Plantinga, *God, Freedom and Evil* (London: George Allen and Unwin, 1974), part I.

[3]*An Introduction to the Philosophy of Religion* (Oxford: Oxford University Press, 1982), p. 23.

[4]*The Enchiridion on Faith, Hope and Love*, trans. J. F. Shaw (Chicago: Regnery, 1961), XI.

[5]*On the Harmony of the Foreknowledge, the Predestination, and the Grace of God with Free Choice in Trinity, Incarnation and Redemption*, ed. and trans. by Jasper Hopkins and Herbert W. Richardson (New York: Harper, 1970), p. 168.

[6]*Summa Theologiae* vol. 25, trans. John Fearon OP (London: Eyre and Spottiswoode, 1969), Ia. 2. 79. 2. A brief defence of evil as a privation is to be found in W. S. Anglin, *Free Will and the Christian Faith* (Oxford: Clarendon Press, 1990), pp. 134–137.

[7]George Morton, *The Divine Purpose Explained* (Philadelphia: Joseph M. Wilson, 1860), p. 84.

[8]*City of God*, XIV. 27.

[9]Jonathan Edwards, *The Freedom of the Will*, Pt. IV. 9. In 'Predestination and Freedom in Augustine's Ethics', in *The Philosophy in Christianity*, ed. Godfrey Vesey (Cambridge: Cambridge University Press, 1989), Gerard O'Daly argues that there is a close similarity between Augustine's and Edwards' views of the will.

[10]Jonathan Edwards, *op. cit.*, Pt. I. 5.

[11]*The Presumption of Atheism* (London: Elek, 1976), p. 96; see also his 'Compatibilism, Free Will and God', *Philosophy*, 1973. Flew has subsequently modified his views. See, for example, 'Freedom and Human Nature', *Philosophy*, 1991.

[12]See, on this theme, William E. Mann, 'God's Freedom, Human Freedom, and God's Responsibility for Sin', in *Divine and Human Action*, ed. Thomas V. Morris.

[13]*Summa Theologiae* vol. 14, trans. T. C. O'Brien (London: Eyre and Spottiswoode, 1975), Ia. 105. 5.

[14]*A Defence of the Secret Providence of God*, p. 251.

[15]*Ibid.*, p. 231.

[16]*Ibid.*, p. 233.

[17]*Ibid.*, pp. 235–236.

[18]*Philosophical Theology* (Indianapolis: Bobbs-Merrill, 1969), pp. 252–253. See also Kathryn Tanner, *God and Creation in Christian Theology: Tyranny or Empowerment?* (Oxford: Blackwell, 1988).

[19]Austin Farrer, *Faith and Speculation*, (London: Black, 1967), pp.

64–65. See also Vernon White, *The Fall of a Sparrow* (Exeter: Paternoster Press, 1985).

[20] Austin Farrer, *op. cit.*, p. 65.

[21] Austin Farrer, *op. cit.*, p. 66.

[22] Austin Farrer, *op. cit.*, p. 194.

[23] Vernon White, *op. cit.*, p. 116.

[24] 'Over-power and God's Responsibility for Sin', in *The Existence and Nature of God*, ed. Alfred J. Freddoso (Notre Dame: The University of Notre Dame Press, 1983).

[25] For example, Peter Van Inwagen, *An Essay on Free Will* (Oxford: Clarendon Press, 1983); Gary Watson (ed.), *Free Will* (Oxford: Oxford University Press), 1982); J. M. Fischer, ed., *Moral Responsibility* (Ithaca: Cornell University Press, 1986); Harry G. Frankfurt, *The Importance of What We Care About*.

[26] Berofsky, *Freedom From Necessity: The Metaphysical Basis of Responsibility* (London: Routledge, 1987), p. 25.

[27] Harry G. Frankfurt, *op. cit.*, ch. 1.

[28] Berofsky, *op. cit.*, p. 31.

[29] Berofsky, *op. cit.*, p. 69.

[30] See, for example, Harry G. Frankfurt, *op. cit.*, p. 23.

[31] Anselm, *On the Harmony of the Foreknowledge, the Predestination, and the Grace of God with Free Choice*, p. 168.

Chapter 8

[1] There is an enormous literature on the free will defence. The modern *locus classicus* is Alvin Plantinga, *God, Freedom and Evil*. It is often claimed that the free will defence is Augustinian, but Nelson Pike argues the contrary in 'Plantinga on Free Will and Evil', *Religious Studies*, 1979.

[2] Alvin Plantinga, *op. cit.*, p. 44.

[3] It could be argued that the fall had metaphysical as well as moral consequences, that it resulted, for instance, in a loss of indeterministic freedom. In a fallen world deterministic conditions are punitive, part of the curse. This is in many ways a neat proposal, but not without difficulties of its own. For example, if unfallen mankind was indeterministically free, then the problem of relating God's knowledge and will to such free actions remains. For instance, if indeterministically free actions cannot be foreknown, not even by an omniscient God, then the fall could not have been foreknown by God.

[4] Augustine, *Enchiridion*, XI.

[5] Stephen Wykstra, 'The Humean Obstacle to Evidential Arguments from Suffering: On Avoiding the Evils of "Appearance"', in *The Problem of Evil*, ed. M. M. Adams and R. M. Adams (Oxford: Oxford University Press, 1990).

[6]Brian Davies, *An Introduction to the Philosophy of Religion*, p. 24.

[7]Trans. D. Magarshack (Harmondsworth: Penguin, 1958), p. 286.

[8]Stephen Wykstra, *op. cit.*; and William Alston, 'The Inductive Argument from Evil and the Human Cognitive Condition', in *Philosophical Perspectives* 5, *Philosophy of Religion*, 1991, ed. James Tomberlin.

[9]Marilyn McCord Adams, 'Horrendous Evils and the Goodness of God', in *The Problem of Evil*, ed. M. M. Adams and R. M. Adams, p. 219.

[10]*Ibid.*, p. 215.

[11]John Hick *Evil and the God of Love* (London: Macmillan, rev. ed. 1977), p. 287.

[12]Augustine, *Of True Religion*, trans. J. H. S. Burleigh (Chicago: Regnery, 1959), S. 39.

[13]Augustine, *The Free Choice of the Will*, trans. Anna S. Benjamin and L. H. Hackstaff (Indianapolis: Bobbs–Merrill, 1964), I. 1. 1.

[14]*Letters of St. Augustine*, trans. Sister Wilfrid Parson SND (Fathers of the Church, vol. 32), (Washington D.C.: Catholic University of America Press, 1956), letter 217.

[15]John Hick, *Evil and the God of Love*, p. 280.

[16]John Calvin, *A Defence of the Secret Providence of God*, p. 274.

[17]For a sharp critique of a notable theologian who attempted such an explanation, see John H. Gerstner, *The Rational Biblical Theology of Jonathan Edwards* (Powhatan, Virginia: Berea Publication), vol. 2 (1992), ch. 22.

Chapter 9

[1]For simplicity of presentation I shall not discuss the middle knowledge justification of the 'no-risk' view separately. The reader may care to work out for himself the operational differences between the 'no-risk' view of providence based upon divine ordination, and that based upon the actualization by God of possibilities involving indeterministically–free human choices.

[2]For example, Ulrich Zwingli, 'On the Providence of God', in *On Providence and Other Essays*, ed. S. M. Jackson and W. J. Hinke.

[3]T. J. Gorringe, *God's Theatre: A Theology of Providence* (London: SCM Press, 1991), p. 66.

[4]*Ibid.*, p. 66.

[5]Donald M. MacKay, *The Open Mind and Other Essays*, ed. Melvin Tinker (Leicester: Inter-Varsity Press, 1988), chapters 6 and 15.

Index